A Long Walk Home

A Long Walk Home

⋘ my own story ⋙

Joan Grindley

iUniverse, Inc.

New York   Bloomington

A Long Walk Home
my own story

iUniverse books may be ordered through booksellers or by contacting:

iUniverse
1663 Liberty Drive
Bloomington, IN 47403
www.iuniverse.com
1-800-Authors (1-800-288-4677)

Because of the dynamic nature of the Internet, any Web addresses or links contained in this book may have changed since publication and may no longer be valid. The views expressed in this work are solely those of the author and do not necessarily reflect the views of the publisher, and the publisher hereby disclaims any responsibility for them.

ISBN: 978-1-4502-2640-0 (sc)
ISBN: 978-1-4502-2641-7 (ebk)

Printed in the United States of America

iUniverse rev. date: 05/14/2010

Preface to "A Long Walk Home"

There are things from my past that I would just as soon forget. I suppose it's that way for all of us. It's what we mean by "baggage" – This *stuff* we carry around with us that weighs our lives down a little or a lot. It is the memory of cruel words spoken, loves lost, relationships ended. It is all our past hurts, both the pain we have experienced and the pain we have inflicted on others.

I have tried to recall both the good and the bad in this memoir but hope I have concentrated on, if not the good, at least the true. There are many things that I still hold deep inside and this is done deliberately. Some things serve no purpose in meeting the light of day. My reason for writing this memoir is first, to conclude the trilogy started with Julia and Emma and second, to allow my children to know the truth and in so doing perhaps understand their mother better. As with my other novels, the surnames have been changed to protect both the guilty and the innocent.

Prologue

The first time I announced that Emma was the second novel in my planned trilogy, with Julia being the first, I knew I would have to come up with a third book. I don't think I fully comprehended then that I was the obvious choice for the heroine, having already covered my grandmother and my mother. That word trilogy is certainly intimidating. When the realization hit me, I knew I could not bring myself to title the novel Joan, so I had to search my brain for an appropriate title.

I decided to begin at the beginning with my earliest memories and move forward through the various stages of my life. Following a brief chain of events heralding my youth in order that my children might relate in some way to some of the parallels in our lives, I chose to begin the real story, as I did with Emma, in my 16th year. As with both Julia and Emma, my life took many twists and turns before it arrived at the peaceful state I like to think of as home, and thus the title of this memoir novel.

Living up to his expectations was the most challenging task of my life. Daddy had written the script for me the day I was born and God forbid I didn't follow it to the letter. I was, of course, ordained to be the smartest, most beautiful, most accomplished young lady that ever graced the planet. Unfortunately, someone forgot to inform my psyche and, more importantly, my creator.

The only human being who ever believed this rubbish, beside my father, was my dear brother Charles who was born five years after me. No matter how hard he tried he could never live up to his parental script but spent his childhood looking up to me as his savior and hiding from my father's wrath. It took many years of coaching before Charles could muster the courage to defy parental authority and be his own man. Thank God, he finally exorcised his demons and made a life for himself.

And what about our mother you may ask. Where did she fit into this drama? The answer is simple. Emma, only daughter of Julia, was an absolute saint – an angel sent from Heaven as an antidote to violence and overbearing fatherly authority. No one could talk down my father except my mother and she did it constantly. She did not always succeed but did manage to save her children many times from our father's anger and resulting brutality. I loved her with a boundless passion and so did my sweet baby brother.

Except for my four children, nine grandchildren, one great grandchild and my one niece, I am the last of the bloodline. This, then, is my attempt to organize my warring memories into a meaningful narrative.

BOOK I

The Early Years

Chapter 1

&

In the beginning

Icame screaming into the world on Memorial Day, 1932, hale and hearty and without any visible impediments.

My first real recollection is of a social nature. I can clearly see myself strolling down the street with two of my girl friends on a Sunday morning decked out in our childish finery consisting of tiny shoulder pocketbooks, scaled to fit our diminutive size, filled with wonderful grownup goodies such as tiny lipsticks, compacts, combs and in mine, a lace hankie. The latter was a hand-embroidered gift from my maternal grandmother, and one of my few treasures. I am a mature three-year old.

My parents are, of course, on the porch of the only house on our side of the street immediately adjacent to the apartment building where I live. From the Zambetti's porch they have a perfect vantage point from which to watch the fashion parade. This delicious event always takes place after church it seems, and I confess I think back on it as a ritual occurrence. I know I was only three, but I distinctly remember feeling like a very grown up young lady with my paten leather "Mary Janes" gleaming in the sunlight. Each of us thought ourselves to be the most beautiful and elegant lady in the world. After walking up the block and down again we are then summoned into Mrs. Zambetti's house where we are called to the kitchen and served milk and cookies and then permitted some time to review the experience we just had. We compare the contents of our pocketbooks and sometimes trade treasured items for ones we think more enticing. I never trade my lace handkerchief.

My next recollection is one that recurred often as a nightmare through my fourth year of life. My mother had allowed me to go downstairs ahead of her prior to an outing. I hear the phone ring as I begin negotiating the stairs, but think she is right behind me. Feeling very independent, I continue down the stairs which end in a small alley at the back of the apartment building.

As I go through the doorway looking for a likely place to await my mother's descent, I see a man coming toward me. I smile up at him but am almost immediately filled with dread. I do not know him. He looks at me in a strange way and then reaches out his hand. Before I can turn away, he grabs me by the shoulders and begins pulling me toward him. I scream and almost instantly I hear my mother's footsteps on the stairs. The man must have heard them too, because he releases me with a great push and begins to run down the alley. The image of this man's face stayed with me for a long time. I remember my mother buying me a special night-light – a tiny pink angel with white wings. I had this special light on in my room for several months before I finally could sleep without it. I wonder in my childish mind if this is a portent of things to come.

When I am almost five my mother enrolls me in tap-dancing classes at a studio on Fordham Road in the Bronx. We have to take a trolley car to get there, and this is almost as much fun as learning to dance like Shirley Temple. The bad part is that my mother's best friend enrolls her daughter, Jeannie, too. I really don't like her at all. We learn all the dances made famous by the Shirley Temple movies, and my favorite is the time step to *Hey Babe, Hi Babe,* from a movie Shirley made with the famous black dancer, Bill Robinson.

When it comes time for the year-end recital, Jeannie and I have to do a duet. This duet, unfortunately, includes singing as well as dancing. We wear matching skimpy pink satin costumes and, even though I don't sing very well, I do love to dance. We are each supposed to sing one verse and join in together for the chorus. I sing my verse and we both sing the first chorus, but when it comes time for Jeannie to sing alone, she freezes.

Instead of singing for her, I just keep scolding her, "Sing, Jeannie, sing; don't just stand there, sing!"

The audience thinks this is hysterically funny and proceeds to laugh and laugh. I, and my parents I might add, are mortified. While I am haranguing Jeannie, she flees from the stage balling like a baby. I just keep on dancing, but never sing another note. That is my last year of tap dancing lessons.

My earliest vacation memory was on a farm when I was six years old. My parents loved the Margaretteville Valley in upstate New York, though farming was about as far from their frame of reference as the moon. In truth, my father was a terrible snob when it came to people like farmers. He classed them with day laborers whom he looked down upon from his lofty ego. For some unfathomable reason the mountains and valleys of New York State held a real fascination for him, and so this particular summer he determined we would summer on a real honest-to-goodness working farm.

Daddy had heard of the farm from a young engineer in his office whose aunt and uncle were the proprietors. They had decided to take in boarders for a few weeks in the summer to supplement their meager income. We were their first visitors.

We left home on a Thursday afternoon to get a jump on the weekend traffic and arrived just after dinner. I remember it clearly because the farmer's wife made such a fuss about giving us a hearty supper after being on the road all afternoon. The smells emanating from the kitchen and that wonderful home-cooked meal stayed with me all evening.

After supper, Mrs. Keane, the farmer's wife, showed us to our rooms. This was the first time I had ever been away from home and sleeping in a room other than my own. I think I expected to share a room with my parents, but this was not to be the case. Mommy and Daddy had a big high-ceilinged room with a fireplace and the biggest bed I had ever seen. It had a top on it – a canopy my mother called it, and it reminded me of a throne from the fairy tales she read to me. My room, on the other hand, was very tiny and located on the opposite side of the hall. It had one small window and, of all things, a crib. I was horrified! I had not slept in a crib for three years now and my nose was definitely out of joint. I did not dare complain to my father, however; I would have gotten a smack for my trouble. I hoped Mommy might notice my predicament and do something to relieve me of this shame. I soon realized that her fear of my father in this situation was as great as my own.

Mommy brought my little suitcase into the room and put it down near the crib. She instructed me to undress and get ready for bed, so I knew I was doomed. I donned my Shirley Temple nightgown, hugged my Shirley Temple doll to me and climbed into the crib. I guess I was more tired than I thought 'cause Shirley and I were asleep almost immediately. Suddenly there was a loud crash. My eyes flew open and I was aware of a pain in the small of my back. Shirley was nowhere to be found and the room was slowly filling with light. I looked up and saw that bars surrounded me. It soon became apparent that I was on the floor. The entire crib mattress had shrugged off its hooks and fallen to the floor taking Shirley and me with it. Shirley, I soon discovered, had flown out of the crib altogether and was staring at me through the bars from the floor just below the window.

I began to take stock of the situation and realized that I was a prisoner in this cavern of bars. I was about to shout for help but thought better of it, knowing my father's reaction to calling attention to myself. I knew I would have to wait for my mother to come and wake me in order to taste freedom again. She would surely set me free with a huge hug and a kiss to make it all better again.

My prayers were answered of course when my mother arrived and took in the somewhat comical situation. After comforting me and lifting me out of my jail, she called the farmer's wife and requested that her "big girl" be given a real bed as soon as possible. The farmer's wife looked a bit chagrined but agreed to make the change at once. I bet her kids slept in cribs until they were ten and thought nothing of it.

I slept much better that night in a grownup bed of my own, and even Daddy accepted the incident with gracious good humor.

The days ahead were full of mystery and new experiences – milking cows, collecting eggs, baling hay and long walks in the fields down to the stream that ran through the property.

On our last morning at the farm I saw an honest-to-goodness snake on my walk to the barn. I screamed and Mommy came running to catch up. She examined the reason for my shrieking and announced it was only a harmless garden snake that would do us no harm. I relaxed and ran on down the path into a field I had not been in before. There were a whole lot of yellow flowers growing in the field and as I ran over to begin picking them, I heard my mother scream. I looked up to see the biggest cow I had ever seen walking toward me. This cow had horns on its head and instilled fear in me the minute I saw it. I stood up, dropped the flowers and began to run. The cow began to run toward me. I ran faster than I ever had in my short life, intent on reaching the gate where my mother was still screaming. Out of the corner of my eye, I saw her open the gate and put out her arms. I ran into those arms and heard the gate slam just as the big-horned cow hit the fence. I was safe but still shaking with fear.

My father arrived momentarily, having heard my mother's scream from the front porch of the house. One look at the bull and then at me made the situation quite clear. He lifted me from my mother's grasp and hugged me tight, a rare show of affection for my father. I hugged him back and, with one parent in each hand, I trotted back to the main house.

I was chased by a bull. What a story I would have to tell my friends.

Chapter 2

A taste of tragedy

One of the most traumatic memories of my early years is of an accident I witness in the rear of our apartment building when I am four and a half. I go back there to play because there is a kind of courtyard with a swing and a seesaw, and my Mother can see me from our kitchen window.

One morning when I am out there swinging I hear someone call me. It is my friend, Claire, who lives on the second floor. She is calling to me from her bedroom window that faces the courtyard. I hop off the swing and walk across the cement pad and stand under her window. I crane my neck to look up.

"Can you come out and play?" I ask.

"No," she sniffles. "Mommy is punishing me for being fresh. She says I have to stay in the house."

She has climbed up on the window seat and is leaning on the screen talking to me. Suddenly, the screen gives way, and the next thing I know my friend is lying on the cement at my feet with blood running out of her head. I scream and scream. A man rushes from the door of the building and comes to where she has fallen. He picks her up in his arms and carries her away. I run after them and follow the man carrying her all the way to the door of their apartment. Just as we reach the door, it opens and he goes inside, slamming the door after him. I am left in the hall in the dark listening to the silence.

Why isn't she crying? I think. *I would be crying if I hit my head.* I race out of the building and into the courtyard again. On the ground beside a small pool of blood is one of Claire's slippers. I grab the slipper and run back to her apartment. I ring the bell and someone comes to the door. I try to explain that this is my friend's slipper, but the person just snatches it from my hand and slams the door again.

I don't know what to do after that; I feel so helpless and scared. I go up the stairs to the third floor where our apartment is and knock on the door. My mother comes to the door. She knows by my face something has happened. I try to explain to her what happened, but she just hugs me to her and says it will be all right. I never see Claire again.

My final recollection of these very early years comes when I am five years old and my baby brother is born. At first I think I am being punished for something because I am not allowed in the nursery to see him. Once I sneak in when my mom isn't looking, but it is so hot in the room (95 degrees I learned later) that I back out gasping for air. I never even get to catch a glimpse of my new baby brother, Charles. This enforced isolation goes on for weeks until my brother gets stronger, and the doctor says he is going to be all right. I hear Mommy and Daddy talking about the fact that Charles is premature and only weighed three pounds at birth. I don't know what premature means, but I know three pounds is pretty small, even for a baby.

I have wanted a baby brother or sister for as long as I can remember. Now I have one, but I just haven't been introduced yet. *Boy, will he be surprised when he discovers he has a big sister.* From the first time I see him, I worship him. I become his protector and defender from that day on. The defender part is mostly because of my Daddy who is very strict and very quick to lose his temper. He likes to punish first and ask questions later. Daddy is still worried about Mommy too. Dr. Kramer told her not to have another baby or she might die. That makes me very afraid that she might go away, and I would not have a mother anymore. I love my Mommy more than anything or anyone in the whole world. I know she loves me too, even though she has a new baby to take care of. I make up my mind to be as much help as I can, so Mommy will never get sick and leave us. My brother Charles becomes a top priority, and I am like a second mother to him even though I am only five. We remain best friends all our lives.

I am amazed now at how much I do recall of those first five years, and I often wonder in what way these events may impact my adult life.

Chapter 3

Middle youth

The fifth year of my life slides into the sixth with a vengeance. Suddenly for a reason that is never shared with me, we move from our third floor apartment on Oradell Avenue in the Bronx to a house on Riverdale Avenue. This area is always referred to reverently by my father as just plain "Riverdale" and the designation " the Bronx" is seldom if ever heard again in our house. I think we have moved to another country because where I had lived for the first five years of my life is never mentioned again.

Being resilient as children are at the age of six, I quickly forget the old and concentrate on the new. The house does not exactly have a yard because only a narrow driveway separates us from the house next door, and the one after that, and so on down the slope of Riverdale Avenue. We do, however, have a small square patch of green grass bordered by a few skinny plants right outside our front door. This is "my yard" I determine, and I bring my tiny child-size chair out there and sit in the sun with my Shirley Temple doll and have tea parties. Sometimes we even invite Sonja Henie who has fallen out of favor with me of late.

I soon discover my neighbors – two boys. One, Karl by name, is my age and his brother, Tim, is closer to Charles's age. What heaven

– a special friend for each of us to play with. Karl and I soon become inseparable.

Six months after we move in Daddy decides we need a dog in the house. Neither Mommy nor Charles and I are consulted. A frighteningly large red chow makes his entrance the next day at the end of a leash held by my father. After surveying his new terrain he adopts the underside of our refrigerator as his special domain. The ice box (as we still call it) is up on legs, leaving just enough room between its base and the floor to contain "King" (my father named him). From that day forward he lives up to his name and is in fact a king in our house, guarding us all, but especially Charles and I, as though we were treasures to be cherished at all cost.

All is well until one day when I bring a friend home after school. Now that I am in first grade, this is a special treat accorded me by my mother. My friend and I are wrestling on the floor, laughing and hollering in gleeful abandon. King mistakes this childish exuberance as a cry for help. He must think my friend is hurting me and I am screaming in pain, because he lunges at her small chest and bites her. All laughing ceases immediately and real cries of pain and fear fill the air. My friend is terrified and so am I. My mother races into the room, surveys the situation, gathers my crying friend into her arms and takes her into the bedroom. Her next move is to call a doctor and my friend's mother. The doctor arrives soon and pronounces the wound superficial, but advises that he will have to report this incident to the Police. Chows, it seems, are allowed only one bite and then they have to be destroyed. It is the law in our city the Policeman explains to us when he comes to take King away.

My friend's mother arrives soon after that and removes her child from our house as fast as she can, spewing invectives as she flees with my friend in her ample arms. I never get to have that little girl over after school again. We see each other in school, of course, but she rarely speaks to me. My father blames me, as usual, for the loss of his prized animal. He never forgives me either.

When I begin second grade, I am allowed to take the bus to school. Mommy drops me at the bus stop after she takes Daddy to the train station. Each afternoon she picks me up at the same place, "the tower," a tall stone edifice alongside the Henry Hudson Parkway at about 231st Street. One morning Mommy drops me off and the bus is a bit later than usual. My hands are cold and my mittens are in my coat pocket. I take the nickel she has given me and put it between my front teeth while I get out the mittens and put them on. A car skids close by the tower, causing me to suddenly draw in my breath. The nickel slides right down my throat. When the bus comes, I hide behind the tower because I am too embarrassed to admit I have swallowed my bus fare.

I stay there all day at the foot of the tower, shivering and growing colder every minute. Finally, after what seems to me a lifetime, I see my mother's car coming around the corner. The bus has not yet arrived to drop the children off. I rush to the edge of the curb to get into the car as quick as possible before my mother realizes I did not just get off the bus. I promise myself I will never tell her, but one look at me told her that something was definitely awry.

As soon as we pull into the driveway of our house, Mommy turns and pulls me into her arms. I blurt out the whole story amid a stream of sobs and "I'm sorry's." As always I was forgiven immediately and treated to a hot chocolate, a warm bath, and more importantly the words, "we won't mention this to Daddy."

One of the happiest and most special memories of my seventh year is that of my mother taking me on the trolley car to the huge movie theatre on Fordham Road to see a Shirley Temple movie. Shirley Temple and the Little Rascals were the only movie stars I was aware of at this tender age. Even though I had given up tap dancing at the insistence of my father, after embarrassing him in public two years earlier, I still idolized Shirley and her dancing ability.

I vowed that one day I too would be a dancer. I sometimes hid behind the door and watched my mother and father dancing in the living room to their Glenn Miller records. They called this ballroom dancing, and for me, it was love at first sight. I never tired of watching them sway together in perfect harmony to the beautiful music. Sometimes Mommy would break into a fast dance she called The Charleston or the Black Bottom. I am surprised to see my usually quiet and docile mother shimmying and gyrating like a crazy person. She is smiling all the while and so is Daddy even though he doesn't join in. They appear together sometimes in something Daddy calls a Varsity Show, for graduates of Columbia University, his alma mater. What a beautiful couple they make – Daddy in his tuxedo and Mommy in a slinky black dress with almost no back and tiny black pumps with heels so high they make her 5'1" frame come almost to Daddy's shoulder. She wears a blue sequined flapper band across her forehead and a black veil covers her long blond hair. I think she is the most beautiful and exciting lady I have ever known.

Chapter 4

Personal trauma

My eighth year is, in many ways, one of the worst of my life. This is the year we move out of Riverdale and into the suburbs of nearby Westchester County. The reason for the move is the result of a horrific experience which I will endeavor to relate. Much of this experience I have blotted out of my memory but some of the details haunt me still.

I am playing outside in my front yard, as I often do on Saturday morning. Our next door neighbor, Uncle Karl as I call him, is baby sitting me while my parents are shopping. Uncle Karl and his wife are my parents' best friends. They play cards together in the evening and spend a lot of time in each other's homes.

Uncle Karl is mowing the grass and cleaning up the yard. I ask him if I may go inside and get a drink of water 'cause it is so hot in the yard. He readily agrees but cautions me against touching anything on the kitchen table. I assure him I won't and go through the side door into the kitchen. I pass the table on my way to the sink. I pause and notice that the table is covered with photographs. They are all face down and I cannot resist taking a peek. I turn over one and then another. I stare at what I see– pictures of naked men and women in strange poses. I do not understand what I see but somehow I sense that they are not nice pictures. I quickly turn them over, but not before Uncle Karl comes into the kitchen. He flies into a rage and begins to berate me for disobeying him.

Then, just as suddenly, he begins speaking to me in a soft gentle way. I have a tiny flashback to an earlier time in an alley with a man smiling at me. Uncle Karl was smiling at me and had hold of my arm. He was propelling me toward the bedroom, muttering what a sweet girl I was. Within seconds he had shut the door and was coming toward me brandishing a small round hairbrush.

"I won't hurt you; I love you." he murmured.

I was so frozen with fear that I could not move as he came closer and closer to me. My head told me to run but my legs just wouldn't obey. He grabbed me and threw me onto the bed. He jumped on top of me and I felt the handle of the hairbrush being shoved under my skirt and between my legs. Suddenly, the sound of the doorbell echoed through the room. It jarred my consciousness and I began to scream. The answering shout was my mother's voice calling my name. I called out to her as loudly as I could between sobs and pulled away from Uncle Karl with all the strength I could muster. He released me with a groan and sank to the floor.

I ran out of the room and straight to the front door and straight into my mother's arms, sobbing as if my heart would break. Mother took in my disheveled appearance and recognized the fear in my eyes. She took me by the hand and led me across the yard and into our front door. My father greeted us at the door. By this time hysteria had overcome me and I was sobbing uncontrollably. My mother held me to her. As I calmed down I tried to tell my father what had happened. I will never forget the look on his face.

Abhorrence and disgust were mirrored there, and all he kept saying was, "What did you do to make Karl so angry? You must have been a very bad girl to get him so upset."

Eventually my mother convinced my father that I had not provoked the incident, and many weeks later the case went to trial. At the tender age of seven I was forced to take the witness stand and tell what happened. As I haltingly tried to describe what happened in between sobs, Uncle Karl was seated in front of me at a table, just staring at me with the coldest, meanest eyes I have ever seen. Several times I lost control and the judge made the bailiff walk me around outside to calm me down. He was a kind man, but he just didn't know what to do with a hysterical seven year old. Uncle Karl was judged criminally insane and sent away to a mental institution.

My father's immediate reaction to this was to move us as soon as he could find a house in the suburbs. In early April we moved into an English Tudor house in a place called Mohegan Heights in Yonkers, New York. It is less than three miles to the elementary school and only a few blocks from the closest high school. My father never mentions the Riverdale incident again. After much love and constant reassurance from my mother the incident begins to fade from my mind. I manage to push it way back into the depths of my memory box and leave it there for many years to come.

I love our new home. This is where I celebrate my eighth birthday, and where I am allowed to see my first movie without my mother – and it isn't a Shirley Temple movie either. I have been emancipated! I am allowed to go with my girl friends that live on the street. We can walk to the village where the theater is through a wonderful park with a lake in the middle, or sometimes one of our parents will drive us. Now, instead of tiny shoulder bags and "Mary Janes," we carry over-sized canvas bags and wear brown and white saddle shoes. We even try to wear the lipsticks we carry, stopping in the park to make ourselves up like grownups. All this "goo" is removed before we return home, of course.

I soon become a real movie nut and start a scrapbook of my favorites – Betty Grable, June Havoc, Debbie Reynolds and the new sensation, Carmen Miranda. I read movie magazines instead of Nancy Drew and write to all my favorites begging for an autographed photo to add to my already burgeoning collection. I am star struck!

Chapter 5

❦

The Good Times

One of the best things that happen this year is that I turn ten and learn to ride a two-wheel bicycle. Daddy takes me out on the street in front of our house. I am very nervous 'cause I know he expects me to learn very fast. Despite my father's expert instructions, I fall off and scrape my knee real bad. I carry his words of disappointment and a bad scar with me to this day.

I make lots of new friends in school and eventually become proficient at riding my bike. We travel all over the neighborhood in a sort of pack, investigating every nook and cranny of our neighborhood – our own little world. There are seven of us and we have promised to stick together forever.

One of my friends lives in a huge brick mansion – like a southern plantation as her mother describes it. There are so many rooms we sometimes get lost and have to regroup in the yard to be sure none of us is missing.

One day, when we regroup, one of us is missing. Annabel is nowhere to be found. The girl who lives here is named Claire and she organizes the search. We start in the library and that's where we make our discovery. Claire shows us a book shelf in the corner that moves. She pushes against it and it slides inward before our very eyes. We are so excited we can hardly stand it. A dark corridor lies beyond the opening and we form a line and begin to walk forward into the dark. Pretty soon we come up against another wall so we lean on it and push as hard as we can. The wall gives way and opens into another room. I'm second in line behind Claire and as soon as we enter the next room I see Annabel sitting on the floor crying.

She looks up and shrieks with joy. "I thought you'd never find me," she cries. "I was so scared."

We hugged her and told her not to worry. We were all together again. We looked around and realized we were in a small bedroom that apparently was not being used by anyone in the household.

"This must be part of the old maid's quarters," Claire announced. "My mommy told me about this part of the house but we don't use it for anything. "Listen," she said, cocking her head to one side. "I think we're near the kitchen. I can hear noise like pots and pans being moved around."

"I wonder if there is another tunnel out of this room and down to the kitchen," I said.

"Let's find out," said Claire. "C'mon, Annabel, we're going to continue exploring. Everyone stay together this time."

She began pushing on the wall as she walked around the room. Suddenly a panel gave way and turned in exposing another tunnel. "There it is," said Claire. "Let's see where it goes." We all followed behind her quiet as mice and within a few minutes we were at a door at the end of the tunnel. Claire pushed open the door and we stepped through one at a time. I looked around and realized we were in a storage room off the kitchen. There were sacks of flour and sugar on the shelves and herbs hanging from the open rafters. Tins and boxes of all sizes were stacked on the shelves too. This was a food pantry which meant the kitchen could not be far away. Sure enough, there was a door across the room. Claire opened it and we all walked into the kitchen. Mrs. Gold, their cook, almost jumped out of her skin and Claire's mother let out a shriek.

"Where did you girls come from?" she asked, a look of amazement on her face.

"We followed the tunnel from the library, Momma," said Claire. "And here we are."

"Oh, my dears, I hope you weren't frightened. I had almost forgotten about those tunnels. Your father and I never told you about them but now I guess an explanation is in order."

Claire's mother explained that the tunnels were used by runaway slaves coming to the north and that their house was actually a stop on the "underground railway."

"Come sit down in the breakfast room, girls, and I'll have Mrs. Gold make us all some hot chocolate. I'll answer all your questions then."

We were fascinated and had many questions for Claire's mother to answer. It was one of the most exciting days of my life. A real life history lesson.

BOOK II

The rest of the tale

Chapter 1

The phone rang just as we sat down to dinner. Daddy grumbled audibly and announced,

"Answer it, Joan, but make it short. You know my rule about phone calls during dinner."

I jumped up from the table and went into the kitchen to take the call.

"Hello," I whispered into the receiver.

"Hi, Joan, can you talk a minute?"

"Make it fast, Al. You know how my father is about interrupting his dinner. What's wrong?"

"Everything" was his reply. "I got drafted today. I leave in two weeks."

My mouth went dry and for a moment I couldn't speak.

"What did you say?"

"I said I got drafted. I'm going to Fort Devon in Massachusetts in two weeks."

"But you can't," I answered. "I gave up college for you. I've only been at Katie Gibbs for six weeks. My father will kill me."

"Joan," boomed a voice from the dining room. "Get off that phone and come to the table."

"I've gotta go, Al. I'll call you back right after dinner."

"But, I need to ……………… "

His voice trailed off as I cut in, "I promise." I hung up the phone and returned to the dining room.

"Was that your beau? Doesn't he know you eat dinner at six o'clock?"

"Yes, Daddy, but something very important came up."

"What could be so important that he had to interrupt your dinner?"

"He got drafted. He's leaving in two weeks."

"What do you mean drafted? That's why you gave up college – to be with him. And now he's drafted?"

Charles Carney pushed his chair back from the table, threw down his napkin and faced his daughter.

"You had your chance, young lady. You chose Al Greene over college. You made your bed and now you are going to lie in it. I will not pay another red cent for your education. When you finish your year at Gibbs, I wash my hands of you. You'll be on your own, and you have Al Greene to thank for that. Maybe next time you'll listen to your father. I told you he wasn't worth giving up college for but you wouldn't listen, and now it's too late. You will be a secretary instead of a teacher and that's all you'll ever be. Now, sit down and let me finish my dinner in peace."

I slumped down in my chair and glanced at my mother. I could see her fighting to keep quiet and noted the pools of water welling in her eyes. She understood the shock I was going through. She put her hand out to pat mine and we exchanged glances. I picked up my fork and poked at the cold food on my plate.

"I'll have my coffee now, Emma," my father ordered without glancing at me. "And a piece of that cherry pie I saw on the counter," he added, putting his napkin back in his lap.

My mother rose from the table, picked up my plate as she turned, and walked into the kitchen. Not wanting to raise my father's ire, I remained in my seat and said nothing. He studied me for a moment and then spoke.

"I'm sorry things worked out this way, Joan, but I'm certain you can understand my position. You'll just have to make the best of the bargain. You'll have a new boyfriend in no time. Mark my words. Al Greene is certainly not the only fish in the sea and I know you can do better. How about picking a rich, educated Catholic boy this time around, eh?"

I did not answer. It was the same old story I'd heard all through high school – rich, educated and Catholic. Daddy seemed to forget that Mother was none of those things, except Catholic, and he had married her for love and no other reason. Why were the rules so different for me?

As if he had read my mind, he went on. "Your mother was one in a million and I knew it the moment I laid eyes on her. No one else would ever be right for me. But you have lots of time yet, and no one is good enough for my daughter, least of all Al Greene with no college, no money and a Protestant to boot. You know I'm right. You just can't see it right now."

Mother walked in with two pieces of pie and put one plate in front of each of us.

"Enjoy your dessert and coffee, Charles. We can talk about this later."

Daddy grunted affably and stabbed at the pie with his fork. I followed suit and silence pervaded the dining room.

As soon as I could, I left the table and went straight to my room to collect my thoughts. I waited till I heard my father turn on the TV to the evening news. I knew his attention would be there for the next hour. I tiptoed down the stairs and into the kitchen where I could use the phone without him hearing me. My mother was washing dishes but would not interfere with my phone call. I dialed the number and waited. It rang at least five times before I heard the click and Al's voice came on the line.

"Hello, is that you Joan?"

"Yes, Al, it's me. I can't talk long but I have to know what happened."

"I got drafted. That's what happened. I never thought they'd catch up to me after all this time. I thought I was free and clear. After all, I'm almost twenty-three, and they're still taking the younger guys."

There was a silence on the line. "Say something, Joan. Talk to me."

"I don't know what to say," I replied. "I never would have given up on teacher's college in New Paltz if I thought you were going in the army. I gave up college to be with you and now you'll be in Massachusetts. I'll never get to see you there."

"I won't be there for long, Joan. They already told me I'll be in the next unit shipping out to Korea. I'm going overseas. There's a war on, ya know. My mom is sure upset. She didn't expect me to get drafted either. Frank's too old now I think, but she thought I was safe too. Guess she was wrong about that, huh?"

"Your brother, Frank, never got drafted. Who ever thought you would. I feel bad for your mom, Al, but right now I feel bad for me." I guess I'll get a job right out of Gibbs and work in New York City. There's no chance of going to college now. My father's made that very clear. Will you write to me?"

"Sure I will and you'll write me back, won't you?"

"Of course I will. How long do you think you'll be gone?"

"Probably two years unless they end the war sooner — that's the rumor anyway. Can we go out this weekend? I want to have some time with you before I leave."

"Of course we can. Maybe Barb and Donny could go with us. It'll be a long time before we're all together again. Call me tomorrow night and we'll make definite plans. I'd better go now before my father comes looking for me."

"I'll call ya tomorrow, Joan. Sleep tight."

The phone went silent and I looked up to see my mother staring at me. I ran to her and she folded me into her arms.

"I'm so sorry, dear. I know what a shock this must be for you."

"I gave up college for him, Mommy, and now I'll never get a chance to go. He'll be gone for two years – two whole years. What am I supposed to do while he's gone – take up knitting?"

"No, dear; you'll go on with your life. You'll graduate from Gibbs and get a great job in Manhattan. You'll make new friends and you may even meet somebody else. I know you'll miss Al, but you're only eighteen and you can't stop living for the next two years. The time will go by before you know it. Whatever happens, Joan, I know you'll be able to handle it. Don't let your father upset you. He just wants the best for you."

"I suppose you're right, Mommy, but I sure wish I hadn't given up college so easily. Being a teacher was always so important to me, and I worked so hard to pass those college entrance exams. Now it's all for nothing and I'll have to settle for being a secretary the rest of my life."

"Maybe not, Joan. Being a secretary could be a stepping stone to something bigger. Think about that when you start looking for a job in the city. You've always loved to write. Maybe you can work somewhere where that talent would be important. Don't be discouraged. You have a whole year to think about what you want to do with your life. Whatever it is, I know you'll make us proud of you."

"Thanks, Mommy. You always did have faith in me. I know Daddy has given up on me, but as long as you haven't, I'll do my best to make you proud."

We hugged and I silently thanked God for the gift of my saintly, wonderful mother.

I had my last date with Al that weekend and it was more than a little difficult for both of us. I had promised myself that I would go down the aisle a virgin no matter what and had made this fact known to Al on several occasions. I suspected he was not a virgin because of his age and obvious experience with several women including Betty Lou, his old girl friend from Roosevelt High School. She was beautiful and had been Miss Westchester the year before Al and I met. She had recently married a guy from Bermuda where she had gone on a trip as part of her prize. She still kept in touch with him I knew, but jealousy was not part of my nature.

Our friends, Barb and Donnie, weren't able to join us Saturday night so, after an early movie and a few beers at Pete's, Al drove the car up county to our old haunt – Nanihagan Road. He parked in our usual spot and began kissing me immediately. He wasn't usually gentle by nature, but tonight he made every effort to take things slow. We started necking and before I knew what was happening, we were at a precipice where I did not want to be.

"I love you so much," were the words he kept whispering in my ear, and I felt myself sliding into submission as these words pounded in my brain. *I love him too so why is this so wrong? Because you may never see him again,* said a voice inside my head and *you don't want to get pregnant.* At the word pregnant my brain clicked in and I saw my father's face in my mind's eye. That was all the deterrent I needed. I pushed Al away and scrambled to retrieve my clothing and set myself to rights. His rage erupted with my first push, and I felt genuine fear for the first time since I'd known him.

"How can you deny me?" he yelled. "I won't see you for months, maybe years. This is all I'll have to remember you."

"If this is the sum total of our relationship, then we don't belong together, Al."

"Well, if that's how you feel than I guess we don't," he snapped back, tucking his shirt back into his trousers.

"I'm sorry you feel that way, but I guess it's best I find out now. Please take me home."

Al slammed the gear shift into drive and wheeled out onto the main road. We drove almost all the way home at breakneck speed and in absolute silence. I could feel the tears welling in my eyes and fought hard to keep them from spilling. I would not give him the satisfaction of knowing how much his attitude hurt and how scared I was at the way he was driving.

He slowed down as we entered the village limits and pulled over and parked by the railroad station. I could feel his eyes boring through me but knew it was better to keep quiet until his rage abated. After about five minutes, I felt his hand on mine and heard words I never thought I'd hear. "I'm sorry, Joan. Really I am. I just didn't know how much I love you and I got carried away. Please forgive me."

I turned to look at him and saw that he really was contrite. "I forgive you, Al, and I want us to part on good terms, not like this. I do love you, but I want to keep myself pure until the day I marry. I'm sorry but that's just how I feel and you have always known this about me. It doesn't mean I don't care about you, it just means I want to wait. I hope you understand."

"I do understand, Joan. Now let's say no more about it. I better get you home before your father sends the cops out after me. Can you come for dinner tomorrow? My mom is cooking all my favorites and it's our last chance to be together before I leave Monday morning."

"Of course I'll come, Al. I'm going to eleven o'clock mass with my parents and then I'll be over. Is that okay?"

"That's perfect. Mom will be pleased. She likes you, you know. I'll see you then."

We pulled up in front of my house. Al leaned over and gave me a lingering good night kiss which I returned with as much fervor as I could without starting another confrontation.

The weekend ended at his house on Sunday with tears, kisses and promises to write. Another phase of my life was beginning.

Chapter 2

As soon as I walked into the lobby at the Katharine Gibbs School on Park Avenue, in New York City, I headed for the lounge and searched the room for my new-found friend.

Maria was usually there earlier than the rest of us because she lived at the YWCA during the week. Her home was in Poughkeepsie, NY, too far to commute every day, so her mother arranged for her to live at the "Y." She went home on weekends and she had come home with me once or twice already. Maria was one of the few friends I had that did not seem to be intimidated by my father, and we hit it off from the very first day at Gibbs.

I spotted her at a corner table with a cup of coffee and headed straight for her.

"Maria, you won't believe what happened. Al got drafted and he's leaving in two weeks for Massachusetts. He thinks he's going to Korea and won't be back for two years. I gave up school for him – can you believe it? What am I going to do now?"

"Wow that is news. I'll bet your father is thrilled. He couldn't stand him was the impression I got."

"He is happy, I guess, but he's madder at me for giving up college for nothing. He won't pay for it now. He made that clear. It's Katie Gibbs or nothin' for me."

"Well, I for one am glad you're here. I don't know if I could get through this prissy school without you. I already hate wearing a hat and white gloves every day to school. Don't worry; you'll just spend lots of weekends with me in Poughkeepsie. We'll have a blast and my boyfriend will get you fixed up with his friends. You'll forget about Al before you know it."

"I really think I'm in love with him, Maria. How can you say I'll forget him so easily? We're going to write to each other – every day."

"C'mon Joan; get real -- every day? With all the homework we have at Gibbs you'll be lucky if you have time to write him once a week."

"You may be right, but I'm gonna try and write more than once a week."

Before Maria could answer, the bell rang signaling the first class of the day.

"I'll meet you back here after fourth period," I said. "I've gotta run and get my steno book out of my locker."

"Okay, see you at lunch."

The bell rang signaling the end of the fourth period class. I stopped at my locker to pick up my lunch and then headed for the lounge. Maria was there already and had saved us a table in the far corner. She was munching on a turkey sandwich and a pile of chips when I sat down.

"Tuna again," I groaned. I think my mother is in a rut. That's the third tuna sandwich this month."

"Stop complaining," joked Maria. "At least it's free and probably a lot fresher than the one I'm eating."

"By the way, Joan, there's a Greek dance at the Commodore Hotel this Friday night. My mother is coming down with Uncle Theo. You're invited to go too, and then come home with us on the train and stay the weekend. Whadya say? It'll take your mind off Al for awhile anyway."

"Thanks Maria. I'd love to if my parents say okay. I'll let you know tomorrow."

My father was doubtful but Mommy convinced him I could do with a change of scene and so I got their permission.

I had spent one previous weekend at Maria's since we met and loved every minute of it. Her mother was a Greek beauty and her Uncle Theo was a handsome and fun-loving chef who taught at the Culinary Institute in Poughkeepsie and cooked amazing Greek entrées.

We arranged to meet them at the hotel after school on Friday. We had dinner at the hotel and I learned to eat *Moussaka* (Greek Lsasagna) and *Spanikopita* (spinach pie). Then we went upstairs to the ballroom. I loved to watch Mrs. Maroulis dance with all the men. Theo danced a special Greek dance with several of the men in a big circle and when it ended they all smashed a plate on the floor. I had never seen anything like it.

We had such a good time and stayed so late that we missed the last train out of Grand Central and had to wait for the "milk train" at six o'clock in the morning. Maria and I slept on the bench in the waiting room while Theo and her mother napped. It was a real adventure.

Maria and her boyfriend, Bobby, were determined to set me up with one of his friends and go on a double date, but none of the boys they introduced me to made much of an impression. I was still pretty hung up on Al Greene.

"You gotta break down and relax, Joan," Maria reminded me. "After all, Al won't be around for two years."

"I know, but I miss him something awful. None of the other boys measure up. They all seem so immature after dating someone five years older than me. Any new guy will have to be pretty special to get my attention. I appreciate what you and Bobby are trying to do but it's just too soon, so stop worrying and have a good time."

"Okay, girlfriend," said Maria, "but I'm not going to take no for an answer forever."

"Guys at home are still calling me," I said. "It's not like I've become an instant wallflower. I just feel disloyal going out with some guy while Al is off defending his country."

"Well, you can be a martyr for just so long. You'll go nuts if you stay home every weekend, but I won't bug you for awhile. You'll come around one of these days. I'm not worried."

We enjoyed our Sunday afternoon together and even did some homework that was due on Monday. We had to get to bed early so we could get the early train to Manhattan on Monday morning.

When I got home on Monday night there was a letter from Al. He had been at Fort Devon for six weeks now and wanted to know if I could come and visit. His brother was going to drive his mom up next weekend and I was invited to come along. We would leave on Friday night and stay in a motel in Massachusetts so we would have the whole day with him.

"It's a family day, and it's probably the last time we'll see our families before we ship out. Please come, Joan. I want to see you so badly."

I ran into the kitchen to read the letter to my mother. "Can I go, Mommy? Do you think Daddy will let me? I may never see Al for two whole years. Please make him let me. Please!"

"I'll do my best, Joan, but I can't promise. You know how he feels about Al Greene. Let me talk to him alone after dinner and I'll see what I can do."

"Thanks, Mommy. It means a lot to me."

My mother came into my room an hour after dinner.

"He said yes, Joan, but only because you'll be with Al's mother and brother. I told him you'd be back Saturday night before curfew and that Frank was a very good driver."

"Oh thanks, Mommy. You're the best. I knew you could talk him into it. I'm going to call his mother right now and tell her I can go."

"Just be sure you don't get home too late on Saturday, Joan. I know Massachusetts is a long drive but your father was very clear. You must be home by midnight."

"But, Mommy – I'm eighteen years old. No one else has a curfew like I do."

"I know that, dear, but it's the old story – as long as you live in his house, you will follow his rules."

I wanted to argue but knew it was not my mother's fault. Charles Carney ruled with an iron hand and it was his way or no way. I swallowed the words struggling to get out and just nodded. I was going to see Al – that's all that mattered.

I dialed Al's number. Mrs. Greene answered on the second ring and sounded pleased to hear my voice on the other end.

"I'm so glad you can join us, dear. We want to leave by five o'clock on Friday so we can get to the motel by ten o'clock. We'll stop on the way to get a bite to eat. I hope that's all right with your parents. You and I can share a room, and Frank will have his own."

"I'm sure it will be okay, Mrs. Greene. Thanks so much for inviting me. I'll be ready by five o'clock"

I hung up the phone and sat down on the bottom step. *It would be hard to sleep tonight. What should I wear? Could he kiss me goodbye in front of his mother? I wish tomorrow was Friday.*

Chapter 3

❦

Frank picked me up at five o'clock sharp and we headed for Massachusetts. We stopped at a small roadside restaurant and had dinner and were back on the road before eight o'clock. Frank drove a little fast but I knew he wanted to get us there by ten.

We pulled up to the motel at ten fifteen and Frank checked us in and got the keys.

You and Joan are in 207, Mom, and I'm in 208, right next door. He helped his mother out of the car and pointed to 207. "Go on in, Mom, and I'll bring your bags. I followed where Frank pointed.

"We'll meet you by the car at seven, Frank, and we'll go pick up your brother so we can all have breakfast together. You have the directions on how to get to the base, don't you?"

"Yeah, Mom, I've got 'em. It's only about twenty minutes from here and Al said he could leave the base by seven thirty.

I slept fitfully – thoughts of seeing Al crowded my mind. We left the motel promptly at seven and arrived at the base just in time to see Al walking up to the guardhouse. As soon as he spied the big green Buick, he ran up to the car. I hung back, not sure how to behave in front of his mother and brother. Al hugged them and then, without hesitation, gathered me into his arms. He kissed me right there in front of them and I could feel the flush rising in my cheeks.

"Okay, okay," said Frank. "Plenty of time for that later. Let's go get some breakfast."

The day passed quickly. Al showed us all around the base, proudly pointing out where his barracks was and introducing us to a few of the soldiers. Before we knew it, it was time to have dinner and to think about returning home. Al suggested a restaurant close to the base and by the time we got served and finished our coffee, it was time to head for home. He excused himself and took me by the hand and led me outside. Frank and his mother discreetly stayed behind.

"I'm gonna miss you something awful," he said as he took my hand.

"I'm gonna miss you too," I answered and lifted my face to receive the kiss I knew was waiting for me.

"You will write to me every week, won't you?"

"Of course I will."

"And you'll wait for me --- you'll still be my girl?"

"You know I will. I'll be so busy with school and then getting a job, the time will go by real fast. You'll be home before we know it."

He kissed me again – long and hard this time. "I guess we better go collect Frank and my mother. I don't want Mom to think I'm ignoring her. Kiss me again before we go back inside."

I did and my head was spinning. We returned to the restaurant where Frank was just paying the bill and getting ready to come outside.

"Say your goodbyes, little brother. I gotta get these ladies back home. I don't want Joan's father breathing down my neck. You know how strict he is."

"I sure do." Al hugged his brother. "Thanks for driving up here, Frank. It really meant a lot to me." He turned to his mother and gave her a reassuring hug. "I'll be home before you know it, Mom, and I'll write every week, I promise."

She released him reluctantly and he turned immediately to me "Goodbye, honey."

"Goodbye, Al, and please be careful and be safe. I'll write as soon as I hear from you so I'll have the right P. O. Box."

I kissed him on the cheek and got into the back seat of the car. I watched from the rear window till he was out of sight and wiped away the tears that were trickling down my checks. I closed my eyes and let my head fall back against the seat.

The next thing I knew Frank was calling my name. We were parked in front of my house.

"Thanks for taking me, Mrs. Greene and, I'll keep in touch."

I looked at my watch and realized with relief that I was not late. I still had ten minutes before curfew. I hurried up the walk and into the house. My mother was curled up on the couch in the living room.

"Thanks for waiting up for me, Mommy. Please go on up to bed now. I'll tell you all about it tomorrow. It's been a long day."

I gave her a hug and headed for the stairs. I dropped onto the bed and could feel the tears welling up behind my eyes. *He's gone,* I thought to myself. *He's really gone and I won't see him for two years. I don't know if I can stand it.*

The attack of angst and self doubt continued as I got ready for bed, but when I turned out the light and snuggled down between the sheets, weariness consumed me, and I fell asleep on the way to the pillow.

Chapter 4

The year at Gibbs went by so fast. Here it was June 1951 and I was preparing to graduate. It had been a tough year and, even though I had passed every course, I was the last one out of the classroom for the typing final. I walked out of the classroom and right into the arms of Maria.

"Well, it's about time you got out of there. I've been finished for a half an hour."

"Don't rub it in, Maria. You know how I get when it's a typing test – I fall apart."

"I know; it's like me in an English exam. My brain just shuts down and I can't even handle multiple choices."

"At least it doesn't make any difference if your hands sweat. I've been sliding all over the keys for the last two hours."

Maria smiled and said, "well, it's all over now and we've done our best. At least you've already got a job offer. I can't believe you got so lucky with your first interview. Just imagine, you're going to be working at ABC-TV right here in New York City. I'd give my eye teeth for a job like that, but I promised my mom I'd get a job in Poughkeepsie. Besides, I really can't afford to live in the City – not with the salary I'd be making. And then there's Bobby. I don't want to be away from him either. We might even get married next year, you know."

"You're lucky too, Maria. At least your boy friend is home. Al is in Korea and probably will be for another year. I've almost forgotten what he looks like."

"He's written you lots of letters though, hasn't he? --and sent you a few pictures too. From the little you've shared with me, he sounds pretty serious about you."

"That's just because there are no girls there. Besides, I don't think I'm the only girl he writes to. I remember him telling me that his old girl friend, Betty Lou, likes writing letters."

"Aren't you jealous, Joan?"

"Not really. After all, I've started dating again - nothing serious, but I knew I couldn't just sit home every weekend. Al may have lost interest in me by the time he gets home. Remember, he's almost five years older than I am and he may want someone more mature."

"Are you nuts?" cried Maria. "You're the most mature girl I know. He's not gonna give you up. Mark my words. I'll bet he comes home with a proposal in his pocket."

"No chance."

"Well, just remember what I said, my friend."

I grinned and we linked arms and headed out of the building into the organized chaos of Grand Central Terminal.

"One more week and we're outa here," I said a bit sadly. "I'm gonna miss seeing you every day, Maria. You've been such a good friend this year. Let's promise to keep in touch and get together every few months at least."

"That's a deal," was the reply. "See you on Monday, Joan." With a wave of her hand, Maria sped across the terminal to catch her train to Poughkeepsie.

I returned the wave and hurried down to the lower level to catch my train to Tuckahoe. My mind began to consider the weekend again. I had a date with Mark. He would be home from Rensselaer Polytechnic

Institute tonight and was taking me to dinner and a movie on Saturday. Daddy liked Mark and never missed an opportunity to reiterate all his good points. He came from a wealthy family, was Catholic and was going to college at RPI to become an engineer, the proudest profession in the world according to Charles Carney.

I liked Mark well enough but didn't share my father's enthusiasm for his potential as a husband. In Al's absence Mark helped to fill the time and he didn't pressure me for sex like some of the other boys I dated. *I guess his being Catholic has its advantages.*

The weekend went pretty much as planned. My date with Mark was uneventful except that he hinted at wanting me to be his girl. He reminded me that he'd be graduating in a few months and planned to work in New York City, so we could continue to spend time together. I didn't encourage him but I didn't say no either. After all, being with Mark was better than sitting home alone on a Saturday night.

The last week at Gibbs was hectic. Maria and I still had to take the shorthand final, and. Maria was waiting for me when she came out of the lab.

"That shorthand final was a killer. I know I only got 110 words per minute, and that was a struggle."

"I managed to get 120," I said, "but 110 is all you need to graduate."

"Thank God for that. When do you start work, Joan?"

"Two weeks from Monday. I'm scared, but I'm really excited too. I'll be in the secretarial pool at first, working for the assistant directors. If I do well there, I can move up to the director's pool. I might even get on TV. The personnel lady said the secretaries sometimes have to fill in on the morning shows if there aren't enough contestants. Wouldn't that be neat?"

"Where do you think you'll work, Maria?"

"Oh, IBM, of course. They're the biggest employer in Poughkeepsie. I've already got an interview lined up."

"Well then, I guess we're both all set. Just be sure to keep in touch."

"You know I will. Are you getting your usual train?"

"No, I have to have one more meeting with my counselor and then I go to the "Y" to get the last of my clothes. I'll take a later train tonight and Bobby will pick me up at the station."

We hugged and promised to call each other over the weekend. It was the end of an era for both of us.

Chapter 5

⁂

The alarm burst through the silence of my bedroom. I sat up and focused on the clock across the room. Seven o'clock it glared. My two-week vacation was over and it hit me with a crash -- my first day of work at ABC-TV.

I felt so grown up as I handed the conductor my monthly commuter's pass. Up and down the car men were playing bridge on lap tables. Some were stern and quiet while others were loud and raucous. There were a few women in the car too, but they were definitely in the minority. I looked around, inspecting the other females. Most wore hats and short white gloves and sported tailored business suits. One young woman across the aisle had on jeans and a turtleneck and looked a bit out of place. *She might be a college student en route to Barnard or NYU uptown.* I winced, remembering the college education I had given up so recently.

The train pulled into 125th Street and sure enough the young girl in the jeans got off. It started up again and before I knew it everything outside the window went black. I strained my eyes against the dark and marveled at the tunnel we had entered. A tiny chill went through me as I realized the next stop was Grand Central Station. From there I took the Shuttle to Times Square and then the 7th Avenue subway uptown to 66th Street. When I got off the subway it was only a short walk to the building that housed ABC on the edge of Central Park.

I entered the huge lobby and took the elevator to the sixth floor. The sign read Programming Department I exited the elevator. I walked to the reception desk and gave the girl my name.

"Oh, you're new aren't you?" said the pretty redhead at the desk. "Down that hall and first door on your right. Just ask for Lorraine and she'll show you where the secretarial pool is. That's where you report in. "Good luck, hon."

I headed down the hall, and as I opened the door marked Program Department, I nearly ran head on into a tall man with a shock of black hair over his forehead.

"Excuse me," I said. "I'm looking for Lorraine."

"Well, I wish it was me you were looking for, young lady, but Lorraine is the short blond over there." He pointed to a desk across the room.

I felt my face flame and stuttered a thank you as I crossed to the desk he indicated. The blond looked up.

"You must be Joan Carney from Katherine Gibbs. We've been expecting you. Welcome to ABC."

"Thanks. I'm happy to be here. Can you tell me where I'm supposed to check in?"

Before she could answer, another tall good looking man entered the room and Lorraine tapped him on the shoulder.

"Hey, Shelley, this is our new recruit, Joan Carney. Take her down to the pool, will ya?"

"It would be my pleasure, Lorraine." He tucked my hand under his arm and led me down the hall. I was rendered speechless and was feeling more than a little intimidated. The hall ended in a large room crammed full of desks and people and was fairly humming with activity.

"Here we are, Joan, and this will be your desk."

Shelley pointed to the desk in front of us covered with piles of papers and a big black typewriter. "Have a seat and I'll hunt up your supervisor."

I surveyed the desk. After closer scrutiny, the piles of paper became scripts -- for TV shows I imagined. Pages of dialog were red marked and the parade of words was palpable. The room was a veritable beehive of productivity. *I'm really a part of the TV world.*

I smiled as Shelley returned with a young woman on his arm. "Joan, this is Amy, your supervisor. She'll get you started and show you the ropes." I turned to face the woman and she eyed me thoughtfully.

"First job, huh? Right out of Katharine Gibbs. Several of our best girls came from Gibbs. You'll do okay." She paused and studied me a moment longer. "Well, let's get you started. These are TV scripts." She pointed to the piles of paper. "They have all been edited by the A.D. assigned to the show and your job is to retype them with the corrections they have indicated. Think you can handle that?"

"Oh, I'm sure I can," I answered with a confidence I didn't yet feel.

"Well then, better get started. I'll be back around noon to take you to the lunch room. Then you'll spend a half hour in personnel before you come back here. See you later."

She hurried off and I picked up the first script on the pile. *The United States Steel Hour*, it read – starring Richard Kiley. *Wow, one of my favorite shows.* My fingers began to fly over the keys. The next few hours flew by.

Amy returned at noon and walked me to the lunch room which was like a huge cafeteria. When we had made our selections and paid for our food, she took me over to a table where a few other girls were sitting.

"This is Joan," she announced – "the newest member of the pool." All eyes turned toward me and every face was smiling. I felt immediately at ease. They all introduced themselves and before I knew it conversation was flowing and I had made three new friends.

"Time to go to Personnel," Amy announced. I stood up and I followed her across the room to the elevator. We got off and she led me into a large, elegantly furnished office.

"Take a seat, Joan. The Personnel Manager will be here in a minute and then I'll leave you two alone. Do you think you can find your way back to the pool?"

"Oh, I'm sure I can."

Just then a stunning older woman walked through the door.

"Hello, Mrs. King. This is Joan Carney, our newest member of the secretarial pool. I'll leave her in your capable hands. See you later, Joan."

The woman walked over and shook my hand. "We're pleased to have you at ABC," she said. "Katharine Gibbs produces some outstanding secretaries, and I'm sure you will be no exception. There is some paper work I need you to fill out but the whole business shouldn't take more than half an hour. I'll have you back at your desk in no time."

She was true to her word and I was back at my desk by one thirty. The pile of scripts had grown slightly, I noticed, but I attacked my typewriter with a vengeance, determined to make a big dent in the pile before I left at five o'clock.

"Why are you still here?" the voice inquired. I looked up into the face of Shelley Hull and grinned. "Well, I'm working, of course."

"But it's five thirty, my dear. No one in the pool works after five o'clock. Didn't Amy tell you that?"

"I lost track of time," I said uncertainly. I just wanted to get this script finished. I didn't realize what time it was."

"Don't sweat it," said Shelley. "You'll go far around here with that attitude, I can assure you." Charlie Dubin loves workaholics and Alex Segal may propose marriage."

"Really," I laughed, "and who are they?"

"Only the two most talented directors in television today. Any A.D. would kill to work with either of them. They're the best in the business right now and ABC's got 'em both."

"Well, I'll certainly remember that, Mr. Hull."

"Shelley, please." When I'm a director then you can call me Mr. Hull."

I stood up and got my purse from the drawer. "Okay, Shelley, that's a deal. See you tomorrow and thanks for your help today."

My feet barely touched the ground as I walked to the subway. *This was the end of my first day and the beginning of a whole new life.*

Chapter 6

By the time the first week ended, I felt like I had been at ABC forever. Everyone was so nice and I seemed to be able to keep up with the work load pretty well. By Friday I had visited most every department, including graphic arts where they made the signs, logos and cue cards used in live programming. I even met one of the graphic artists, and from the way he smiled at me, I was sure I would see him again.

I had always loved the theater and working in live TV, I imagined, was almost like that. I visited the prop room, sound effects, and wardrobe and even got to peek into one of the studios while a rehearsal was going on.

It was the most exciting place. Every day brought a host of new challenges and new scripts. I made friends with one of the other pool secretaries – Kay. She took the train out of Grand Central every day to Connecticut. We started taking the subway together and discovered that we both loved the theater. We decided to save our money to get tickets to a Broadway show. We'd have dinner in Manhattan before the theater. I was excited at the prospect of a night out in Manhattan.

The two biggest hits in 1951 were *The King and I* with Gertrude Lawrence and Yul Brynner and *Call Me Madam* with Ethel Merman and Russell Nype. What a tough decision that was. We talked it over endlessly and finally decided on *Call Me Madam* by Irving Berlin -- a musical satire on politics, foreign affairs and an American abroad. It had been running since October 12, 1950 and was playing to a sold-out house. The critics had been raving about George Abbot's direction and also the new choreographer, Jerome Robbins. And so the decision was made. As soon as we had our $3.60 each, we headed to the box office on our lunch hour. We were able to get the next to the last row of the orchestra for a Thursday night two weeks hence.

We were thrilled beyond words. We went back to work clutching our tickets like they were rare gems. All that was left now was to select a place to eat dinner before the show.

When I got to work the next morning, I couldn't wait to tell Shelley about the tickets and ask him to suggest a place for us to have dinner. As soon as he walked in, I waved him down.

"Kay and I got theater tickets and in the orchestra too. Isn't that exciting?"

"It sure is, but tickets to what show?"

"Oh, of course," I laughed. "*Call Me Madam* at the Imperial. "Where should we eat, Shelley? Kay and I don't know anything about the restaurants in the theater district. Any ideas?"

"Can you splurge a little?" he asked with a wink. "The Café Des Artistes is the place to go. You girls will love it. It's right on 67th Street a few blocks from work and from there you can get the subway to the Imperial on 51st. All the important ABC people go there," he added. "It's the best."

"Can we afford it?" I asked. "We're only secretaries, remember."

"If you can afford the theater, than you can afford this. Believe me, Joan, it's worth it."

"Okay, Shelley. I just hope we won't end up doing dishes for our dinner."

The two weeks flew by and here it was the night of our dreams. We both came to work dressed just a bit fancier than usual and most of our cohorts teased us, thinking we had a double date that evening. I assured them they were wrong. At Shelley's urging we had also made dinner reservations at the Café des Artistes for six o'clock.

When we walked into the restaurant, my breath caught in my throat. I had never been in such a fancy restaurant in my entire life. My father never took my brother and I out to a restaurant except on very rare and special occasions. I think I may have been in a restaurant twice in my life before then. Kay admitted this was a first for her too. I gave the maitre de my name and we followed him across the beautiful dining room to a tiny banquette in one corner. He seated us and ceremoniously placed huge linen napkins in our laps.

Before we could recover from this elegant service, a young waiter arrived at the table with menus and a wine list.

"May I get you ladies something to drink?" he inquired with a slight French accent.

Shelley had warned us about the price of alcohol so we already determined that we would not imbibe this evening.

"I'll have an iced tea," said Kay. "And I'll have water with lemon, please. " I added.

"Very good," said the handsome young waiter.

Pleased with our performance thus far, we began to peruse the large, leather-bound menus.

"Boy, dinner will be more than the theater," commented Kay. "The selections sound delicious, but I don't know what half of them are. How is your high school French, Joan?"

"A bit rusty so I'm going to order one of the least expensive items, but not the cheapest," I responded. "We don't want them to think we're poor and don't belong here."

Kay giggled. "We're not poor. It only took us two months to save up for the tickets. I think I'll try the Chicken Cordon Bleu. It sounds so French. I wonder what's in it."

"Oh, that's chicken with ham and cheese inside," I replied with authority gleaned from one of my mother's fancier cookbooks. On a roll, I continued. "I'm gonna have the chicken franchaise. That means it's lightly breaded and served with a lemon butter sauce. All the entrées come with vegetable and a baked potato so we'll have plenty to eat."

We began to study the walls around us. They were covered with beautiful oil paintings and brass sconces which shed a soft light. Small bouquets were on every table and large vases of flowers were placed seductively on the sideboards scattered around the dining room. The room seemed to be right out of the French Renaissance.

"I'm so glad Shelley recommended this place," said Kay. "I've never been anywhere so elegant before."

"Me neither," I agreed, "but I have a feeling this won't be the last time."

"I hope you're right 'cause I sure could get used to this."

The waiter arrived bearing a breadboard with a large loaf of very dark bread. Next to that was a bowl of ice in which several pats of butter bloomed like tiny sunflowers.

In what seemed only minutes, he returned carrying two large plates of food.

As we were finishing our meal, I glanced at my watch and realized it was seven o'clock. "We've gotta get going, Kay, or we'll miss the curtain." I called for the check.

"If we don't tip too much, we might have enough for a cab back to Grand Central after the show," suggested Kay.

"Good thinking," I agreed.

The check came. I looked at it and turned to Kay, but I could hardly speak. Perspiration was forming on my brow and I could feel a sense of panic.

"It's a bit more than I thought," I muttered. "How much have you got, Kay?"

She opened her wallet and pulled out a five dollar bill and two ones. I had two fives stashed in my change purse.

"If we tip ten percent, we'll just make it with enough left over to take the subway. Thank God we have tickets for the train home. We'll have to walk to Grand Central from the theater, but we can use the exercise."

We paid the check and decided to make a stop at the ladies room before heading for the subway. This room proved to be almost as elegant as the dining room. The walls were covered in *toile* and the counters were marble with gold plated fixtures. There was a maid on duty in this elegant rest room and I was embarrassed not to be able to put even a small tip in the plate she proffered. We raced to the subway on the corner and a train was coming in just as we got to the platform.

"We made great time," I said as we crossed the street to the theater. "It's just seven forty-five. Let's go in and find our seats."

We handed our tickets to the usher, clutched our Playbills, and sat down. We were pretty far back in the orchestra but the Imperial was not one of the largest theaters, so we still had a good view of the stage. We surveyed the audience and marveled at some of the elegantly dressed people sitting around us. Kay looked up toward the balcony and remarked that it was packed too. There didn't seem to be an empty seat in the house. When the orchestra began the overture, I could feel chills running up and down my spine.

I'm here. I'm actually at a Broadway show. I just can't believe it. How did I get so lucky?

Chapter 7

Although a bit tired from lack of sleep, I was still on a high from the show the night before. I found myself humming as I waded through the pile of scripts on my desk. My phone rang. I picked it up and propped it on my shoulder. It fell to the desk with a bang when I heard the voice on the other end announce, "Come to Studio 2A at once. We need another contestant for Market Melodies and you're elected."

The phone went dead and I panicked. "I'm gonna be on TV – today – now," I said out loud to no one in particular.

"What did you say?" Kay asked from the desk behind me. "You're gonna be on TV?"

"Yes. They just called me from downstairs. Please call my mom, Kay, and let her know. She'd never forgive me if I didn't tell her so she could watch."

"Sure, no problem. Hurry up now before they change their mind -- and break a leg," she added.

I ran for the stairs and took them two at a time to the second floor. I entered the theater and was immediately corralled by the makeup mistress. As the girl poked and prodded my face and fluffed my straight hair, I saw Shelley Hull coming around the corner. He was grinning from ear to ear.

"How's the star this morning?" he mused.

"Did you do this? Did you arrange to get me on this show? I know you're the associate director, but why me for heaven sake?"

"Because I thought you'd enjoy it and we could use a good looking blond in this audience today."

"What do I have to do? I've never even seen this show."

"It's a simple quiz show and you win prizes like groceries and house slippers. Just follow Dave Murray's lead – he's the emcee, and I'll be cuing all contestants from the sidelines. Not to worry, hon; it's a piece of cake."

An hour later we were on the air and I was as nervous as a cat in a dog kennel. Two contestants went on before me – a middle-aged lady weighing about 200 lbs. and a construction worker from the South. The lady went out with two bags of groceries and a pass to three TV shows.

Then it was my turn. I had been told not to say I worked for ABC but merely that I was a secretary in New York City. Dave asked me some simple questions about homemaking and cooking, and surprisingly, I knew all the answers. Dave had each contestant spin a big wheel. They had a chance to win up to $100. No one had won more than $10 that morning, but when I spun the wheel it stopped on the $100 mark. I was ecstatic and so was the audience. I left the studio with a bag of groceries, some miscellaneous goodies and a check for $100.

When I got back to my desk I was greeted with raucous applause from my fellow workers.

"Nice goin', they shouted in unison. "You're a celebrity now."

"I hope my mom was watching," I said.

"I called her, Joan, so she knew you were on," Kay assured me. "It's lunch time now, so let's go to the cafeteria and celebrate" She grabbed my hand and we headed for the door.

Later in the week I got another opportunity to be on the set – not as a contestant this time but as a program assistant for Shelley Hull during a rehearsal for the *United States Steel Hour*. It was being directed by the famous, Alex Siegel, and Shelley was A.D. on the show. He was as excited as I was. "Working under Alex doing live TV is almost as exciting as working on Broadway," he assured me.

All my adolescent life I had worshipped and adored movie stars. Not so much for their beauty as for their ability to live so many lives through their roles in the movies. I devoured movie magazines and had sent away for signed glossies of all my favorites. I even got a medical excuse from gym in my senior year in high school to get a job as cashier at the local movie house.

Hollywood greats were attempting to break into this new medium of television. Performing live was quite a challenge after the movies which permitted retakes as often as needed. In TV, once the words were out of your mouth, they were cast into celluloid history.

One of my favorites, Nina Foch was starring in the United States Steel Hour. She arrived on the set perfectly groomed, looking every bit the elegant lady I had always admired. She read the first scene with her co-star and was abruptly stopped by the director. Alex came down onto the stage and explained how he wanted her character to react. She did not agree with his suggestions and before long, they were exchanging some choice four letter words. Alex had tried to be polite but Miss Foch did not spare the rod. She let him have it in the choice vernacular of a longshoreman, and he reacted accordingly. My beautiful, elegant Nina fell off her pedestal with a resounding crash while Alex Siegel became a new idol for the intrepid Joan Carney.

Several months later I met the infamous Tallulah Bankhead. I had dreaded her arrival on the set with a passion. Her reputation preceded her, and I was terrified of this alleged mysterious, cold and unyielding diva.

She strode onto the set, more like a man than the beautiful woman she actually was, and shouted "I am delighted to be here. Let's get to work."

Everyone was rendered silent except the director, Charlie Dubin, known for his patience and sensitive nature.

"And we're delighted to have you Tallulah," he shouted back. "And by all means, let's get to work."

She grinned and came over to me. "Hold my hat, will you, *dahling*? I need to feel some wind in my hair."

I muttered something unintelligible and gingerly took the hat from her outstretched hand. At the end of the rehearsal she again came over to where I was sitting, checking the prop list.

"I've come for my hat, my dear, and now how about some lunch? I feel the need of some fresh, young company. Will you join me?"

Flabbergasted by the invitation, I mumbled my assent. We left the building and headed for the local hangout for people from ABC – Healey's Bar and Grill. Tallulah did most of the talking and I was an excellent listener. I was enthralled by her company and was never afraid of her again.

Last, but not least, in the meeting-movie-star department, was Al Jolson. After a year at ABC I was promoted to private secretary to Charles G. Mortimer, Director of TV Programming. In this capacity I often accompanied my boss to meetings with perspective celebs whom the network was considering for new shows they were planning.

The meeting with Mr. Jolson was set for one o'clock. He arrived twenty minutes late and seated himself in the conference room across from my boss, who was more than a little agitated at his lateness. Mr. Mortimer began explaining the pitfalls of certain types of sponsorship. "You've got to pick a product that belongs on a family-type show, Al," he explained. Jolson was not happy with the sponsorship possibilities and said so in no uncertain terms. To punctuate his dissonance on the subject he took the huge Cuban cigar out of his mouth and ground it out on the beautiful mahogany conference table. He then stood up and strode from the room.

This was the "beloved Al Jolson" I had heard so much about who sang about his mammy? I was appalled and said so to my boss as the door slammed in the background. Charles merely shrugged and said,"Celebrity is a license for outrageous behavior in otherwise ignorant people." I saw no reason to disagree, and my attitude toward celebrities was inexorably changed forever.

I loved my job and, though I took on more and more responsibility, I was not feeling fulfilled. Writing had always been my passion and I was getting little or no opportunity to test that skill at ABC. So, when I got an offer from Young & Rubicam, one of the most prestigious ad agencies on Madison Avenue, I took it. Leaving Charlie was a tough decision but I knew I had to try my wings, and he understood. The parting was amicable. I left two weeks after giving my notice.

Chapter 8

I took a week off to clear my head and reported for duty at Young & Rubicam at 9:00 a.m. I was hired as an assistant to Gerry Engel, chief editor on staff. One of her major responsibilities was to provide a cooking column for their prestigious client, The New York Herald Tribune. My first assignment was to write that column under the nom de plume of Clementine Paddleford.

"Cooking column?" I exclaimed. "You want me to be Clementine Paddleford?"

"That's the assignment. Take it or leave it," said Gerry.

"I'll take it," I said. And so for the next six months Joan Carney became Clementine Paddleford. I hounded my mother for ideas and then finally called my grandmother, Julia, in New Jersey to get some fabulous Hungarian recipes like stuffed cabbage, chicken paprika and consommé with Tokay wine.

All went well until Grandma ran out of recipes and I got bored with being Clementine. I got a phone call from Bill Traum, Director of Town Hall of New York.

I had worked on a show while at ABC called *Town Hall of the Air* which was actually filmed at the famous Town Hall on 43rd Street. The format was mainly debates between noted politicians and the show had garnered a great following. Bill needed an assistant and script editor and offered me the job. Almost without thinking, I took it and agreed to start in two weeks. I gave notice to Gerry who did not take it well.

Town Hall opened up new avenues for me. I had never had much to do with politicians and had always been a Republican. My father had told me I was at a rather early age and in my non-political youth I never found a reason to disagree. I soon found hearing two sides of a debate and being able to form my own conclusions a fascinating experience. Eventually I became a political independent and was inordinately proud of my new stance. Town Hall educated me and gave me the ability to consider all sides of issues affecting more than my own small world.

Speaking of which, I will always remember a hot summer day when a brazen pigeon lobbied his way into my office through a slightly open window facing 43rd Street and harassed me for almost an hour. I was hard at work editing an important senatorial debate script. The A/C had been turned off due to an unprecedented electrical failure, and I opened the window to get some much needed air. He literally snuck under the sash of the barely elevated window and began careening around the room, wings flapping and feathers flying. Before I could raise the window and coax the terrified bird onto the sill to make his exit, he had shed half his feathers and managed to leave a message on the open pages of my formidable script.

Bill and I had a good laugh over this and I made certain never to open a window again.

I lasted nine months at Town Hall before getting restless again. Bill was a great boss but seemed to want more from me personally than I was prepared to give. A call from my ex-boss at ABC, Charlie Mortimer, in the summer of 1953 had me making a move once again. He wanted me back and the offer was too good to refuse. I would not only be editing scripts but would be assigned a show one night a week and would be responsible for the scripts and the cue cards for that show. I couldn't resist so once again I gave two weeks notice and was back riding the subway to West 66th Street.

I loved the new job and when I found myself assigned to *Richard Diamond, Private Eye*, starring David Jansen, I was ecstatic. The sponsor was Mogen David Wine and they were just as particular about their commercials as they were about their product. As it turned out, Shelley Hull, now promoted to a director, was also assigned to this show. I was thrilled to be working with him again and made certain that all the commercials were integrated exactly as he requested. He was happy; the client was happy; and so was I. The job seemed to get better every week. David Jansen was a pleasure to work with and even the sponsor seemed to rely on my increasing expertise.

Almost as soon as I returned to ABC, I began dating Johnny Elgin, an artist in the Graphic Arts Dept. I met him when I first joined ABC but had only spoken to him on rare occasions. He lived in Manhattan so we started going out for dinner before *Richard Diamond* went on at nine o'clock. Johnny was doing the graphics for the show so he had a personal interest in it too. Then he asked me out on a weekend. This meant he would have to drive or take the train to Westchester in order to date me. I was impressed. He didn't own a car but said he would borrow one from a friend and would pick me up at seven o'clock. I was to plan where we would go as he knew nothing about Westchester nightlife.

Johnny arrived about five minutes early on Saturday night. I met him at the door and invited him in to meet my parents. My mother greeted him warmly, but my father was his usual arrogant self. Before he could give Johnny the third degree, I got my coat and steered him toward the door.

"Sorry to rush off, Daddy, but we have dinner reservations and I don't want to be late."

"Well," harrumphed my father, obviously annoyed at being cut short in his interrogation. "See that you bring her home on time, young man."

My mother smiled and kissed me on the cheek. "Have a wonderful evening," she said.

"We will, Mommy, and I won't be late; I promise."

"Goodnight Mr. and Mrs. Carney," Johnny nodded as he opened the door for me and led me down the stairs to the car.

The evening went well. Dinner was delicious and Johnny made conversation easily. I considered it a complete success until we got back in the car which he had parked in a dimly lit lot next to the hospital across the street. Suddenly the gentlemanly Johnny became a sex-crazed animal. I was thoroughly unprepared for the onslaught that followed. Before I knew what hit me he had his arms around me like a vise and was kissing me hard on the mouth. I pushed him away and complained loudly.

"Hey, what do you think you're doing? We hardly know each other. This is our first real date and will probably be our last if you're going to act like this."

He looked up at me, amazed. "We've been dating in the City for weeks now, Joan. What did you expect? After all, I drove all the way up here to Westchester to be with you. Don't I deserve a little reward?"

"A reward? You call this a reward? You mean I have to pay for the pleasure of your company just because you drove up here from New York City? Well, guess again, Johnny; just take me home."

He looked at me coldly, moved back behind the wheel and turned over the engine. We drove home in silence and I got out of the car as soon as it pulled up to the curb.

"Goodnight, Mr. Elgin, and thank you for a lovely dinner," I said through gritted teeth, and stepped out of the car. He made no effort to stop me. As soon as I started up the steps to the front door, he had the car in gear and was driving away.

I gave little thought to the loss of Johnny Elgin, although I did make a point of not visiting the Graphic Arts Dept. for the next few weeks. My friend, Mark, had been home from college for a week and he had helped keep my mind off the unpleasant incident.

The phone rang right in the middle of dinner on Wednesday evening. My father glared at me.

"Get the phone, Joan, and if it's for you, tell them to call back later."

I got up from the table and went into the breakfast nook to take the call. Static pierced my eardrum as I picked up the phone.

"Hello. Who's calling?" The static subsided somewhat and an operator came on. "Will you accept a collect call from Corporal. Greene?"

"Corporal. Green? Of course, I'll accept it. Al, Al, is that you?"

"Yeah, Joan. It's me. I'm calling from California. I'll be home in three days."

"Three days? How long can you stay?"

"For good, Joan. I'm being discharged tomorrow. I'm all done with the Army. I'm flying into Idlewild Airport on Saturday. Can you come with Frank and Mom to pick me up?"

"For good? You're out of the Army and you're coming home to stay? I can't believe it."

"It's true. I swear it. I'll be there on Saturday. Please come to get me. I want so much to see you. I've waited so long for this day. I have a surprise for you too. Please, Joan, say you'll come."

"Of course, I'll come. I'll call your mother right away and let her know. I'm so excited, Al. I don't know what to say."

"Just say you're glad I'm home and that you'll see me on Saturday. That's all I need to hear."

"I am glad you're home and I can't wait till Saturday. Bye for now."

"Bye, Joan. See you on Saturday."

I returned the phone to its cradle and leaned against the wall. *He's home, he's really home.*

"Joan, come back in here and finish your dinner," my father shouted from the dining room. "Your food's getting cold."

"I'm sorry, Daddy, but that was Al – Al Greene. He's getting out of the Army and is coming home on Saturday. I'm going to drive out to Idlewild with his mother and brother to pick him up. Isn't that exciting?"

"Exciting is not the word I would choose," said Charles Carney. "I thought we were rid of that young man forever. Now he's back again, is he? Well, I won't like him any better now than I did before he went in the Army, probably less. Don't tell me you're going to start up with him again. What about Mark and that nice Elgin boy?"

I almost lost it when he mentioned Johnny Elgin. *Boy, if you only knew!*

"Let's not jump to any conclusions, Daddy. I'm just glad he's home from Korea safe and sound and you should be too."

My mother grinned at that last statement and waited for her husband to comment. He chose to ignore the remark, however, and pushed back his chair. I stayed put so I could have a chance to talk to my mother in private.

"Can you believe it, Mommy? He's really home. I'm gonna call his mother now and tell her I'll be coming with them on Saturday. Is that okay?"

"Of course it is. Please tell her how happy I am that her son is home. She must be so pleased."

I made the call to Al's mother and then went up to my room to be alone and collect my thoughts. A million things went through my mind. *How would he look? Would he be different? What would we talk about? What would I tell him about Mark? What would I tell Mark for that matter? How could I wait until Saturday?*

Chapter 9

Saturday arrived cool and clear and full of promise. I was up early and ready to go at least an hour before Frank Greene was to pick me up to go to Idlewild Airport. I was so nervous I couldn't sit still. Fortunately, Daddy had left for the golf course an hour earlier so I didn't have to face him and a further interrogation this morning. I tried to settle down to a cup of coffee and some toast but was so jittery I spilled the coffee.

I was intent on wiping up the mess when my mother entered the kitchen.

"Good morning, Joan, and how are you this lovely day?"

I ran to her, "Oh, Mommy, I'm so excited I can't sit still. I can't even pour a cup of coffee without spilling it. I'm a nervous wreck." I sank back into a chair, my head in my hands.

"Calm down, my darling. Frank will be here soon and you'll be on your way. You'll have a whole hour to compose yourself on the way to the airport. You look lovely, by the way. Finish your toast and coffee. You'll feel better with something in your stomach besides butterflies."

Mommy got another mug from the cupboard and filled it with coffee before pouring more into my cup. She sat down next to me at the table and put her arms around me.

"It'll be fine, honey. I promise. Just remember it's been two years since you've seen Al so he may have changed a bit. War can do that to a man, you know. Just be prepared and, above all, be happy. You've been looking forward to this for quite a while and now it's here."

Before I could answer, the doorbell rang. I ran to the front door.

"Hi, Frank. I'm ready."

I grabbed my jacket and shouted, "Goodbye" over my shoulder to my mother. Mrs. Greene was in the front seat and she looked like she had been crying.

"Good morning, Mrs. Greene. This is certainly an exciting day, isn't it?"

Anna Greene sniffled a response and we all settled back for the ride to Idlewild.

Frank tried to make small talk but was not having much success. I stared out the window and was so caught up in my own thoughts that I actually saw nothing. Suddenly Frank's voice broke through my reverie.

"Here we are, ladies. He's coming in to Gate 7 which is right across the street. The plane should be landing in about fifteen minutes. Let's cross over and go into the terminal over there."

Frank pointed to the main doors of the International Terminal. He grabbed his mother's arm and steered her in the direction of the terminal. I followed close behind. We made our way to the waiting room at Gate 7 and found seats along the huge glass window that faced the field. The waiting room was overflowing with families all waiting to greet their sons after a long separation. A voice came over the loudspeaker.

"Ladies and Gentlemen, flight 403 has just landed and the passengers will be disembarking momentarily. Please move away from the door so that the flight attendants may clear the way."

I stood and took a place next to Mrs. Greene. I could feel the crowd pushing from behind. My hands were shaking and my stomach felt like it was rising into my mouth. Suddenly a cheer rose from the crowd and one woman ran forward and clutched at the young soldier who was coming through the door. I could not see over the heads that pushed in front of me, but realized that Frank and Anna Greene were being pushed ahead by the surging crowd. I leaned up against a post for support and then I saw him. He was hugging his mother but looking over her shoulder frantically.

"He's looking for me," I said out loud to no one in particular. I tried to move forward but the crowd was too strong so I backed up against the post. Then I saw him coming toward me with his arms open. I pushed forward and felt his arms close around me.

"I'm home," he said. "I'm really home."

"Welcome home, Al," was all I could think of to say.

He dragged me along through the crowd of well-wishers to an open space at the edge of the waiting room. Frank and his mother followed close behind. Anna Greene was wiping her eyes and I wondered for an instant why I wasn't crying.

"You look wonderful," I blurted out. "And you've gained some weight."

"Yeah," Al agreed grinning. "The Army tends to fatten you up. You look wonderful too, Joan. Thanks for coming out to meet me."

"Listen, brother, we're right across the street so let's get your luggage to the car and we'll head for home," said Frank pointing to the sign that said Baggage Claim.

"Okay by me," said Al grabbing my hand. We all hurried to the escalator and went down to the baggage claim area. "Stay here, girls," said Frank and pointed to two seats against the wall. "Al and I will get his gear and be right back."

Anna and I sat down where Frank indicated and just watched the chaos going on around us. Everywhere we looked, people were laughing and crying, hugging and kissing. It was like one huge reunion. After about ten minutes Frank and Al came back through the crowd carrying two duffle bags and what looked like a huge canvas laundry bag.

"I brought back a few goodies from Japan," he said with a grin, pointing to the canvas bag. "We're gonna have Christmas early this year."

Anna smiled at her son and gave him a peck on the cheek. I stood by quietly, not wanting to get between mother and son.

"Okay guys," said Frank. "Let's head for the car. I'll lead the way."

We went through the main doors and crossed to the parking lot. Frank popped the trunk and threw in the duffle bags. "Easy with the other bag," Al said. "It's got breakables in it."

"Not to worry, brother. I'll treat it with tender loving care."

Al sat in the back and held my hand all the way home. He talked mostly to Frank and his mother telling them about the trip home and asking questions about his friends and their home town. Then he turned to me.

"I saved all your letters," he said.

"I saved yours too," I answered. "I still can't believe you're here, and you're not going away again."

"That's the best part," he answered. "I'm sure glad you waited for me, Joan. That makes it all worthwhile."

He turned my face to his and kissed me full on the mouth. I thought I would die with the sheer joy of it.

Chapter 10

Sunday dawned cool and crisp and full of promise. I was awake and out of bed before eight o'clock. We always went to ten o'clock mass and today would be no exception. Al's family didn't go to church and besides, I was sure he would sleep late on his first morning home. I wanted to be home before noon in case he called. I couldn't wait to see him again.

The phone rang about ten minutes after we got home. "I'll get it," I yelled.

"Hi, Joan. It's me. Can I see you this afternoon? Frank's letting me use the car and I can be there in half an hour. Whaddya say?"

"Yes, Al, but just give me a minute to check with my mother."

"Sure," was the reply. I raced into the kitchen looking for her. She was at the stove already, starting to prepare Sunday dinner.

"Mommy, Al's on the phone and he wants to pick me up in half an hour. Is that okay?" I looked at her anxiously.

"You're in luck, Joan. Daddy has a golf game today so he won't mind if you're not here. We're having dinner tonight instead of the middle of the afternoon so just be home by six and there won't be a problem."

"Thanks, Mommy." I gave her a quick hug and raced back to the phone.

"I can go out, Al, but I have to be back for dinner at six -- okay?"

"Not a problem," was his response. "I'll be there in half an hour to pick you up."

I hung up the phone and hurried to my room to check my image in the full-length mirror. The grey slacks and burgundy sweater seemed appropriate. I ran a comb through my hair and freshened my lipstick.

I hadn't seen my father since we got home from church. I noticed his bedroom door was closed so decided he must be changing into his golf clothes. I prayed Al would get here before he came down stairs. That would avoid a lot of unpleasantness. My father didn't care that Al had been defending his country for the past two years. His only concern was this young man's desire to date his only daughter. Al Greene was not my father's choice for a perspective suitor.

The door bell rang and I flew down the stairs. For a moment I didn't recognize him out of uniform. He smiled and reached for my hand. I gave it to him without hesitation. "Goodbye, Mommy," I yelled over my shoulder and closed the door behind me.

"Where are we going?" I asked.

"How 'bout our favorite diner for burgers and fried onions? I hope they still make 'em the way they used to."

"That sounds swell. I haven't been there for ages. It just wasn't the same . . . ." My voice trailed off.

"Maybe that means you missed me," Al filled in and pulled me closer to him in the car. "After that we're gonna drive up to another of our old haunts – Nanihagan Road." He paused, waiting for a reaction.

I felt my face flush at the mention of our old parking spot. We had some pretty close calls on that road I recalled. I didn't answer.

"I need to talk to you – in private," Al said. "That's one place I know we can be alone."

I nodded and sat back against the seat as we pulled into the parking lot of the diner. The place was pretty crowded but we managed to find two stools at the counter. Al ordered for both of us and grinned when the food was put in front of us.

"I've been dreaming about these burgers," he said, and took a huge bite. "And I'm not disappointed," he added still grinning. "They're just as good as I remember."

I launched into my burger with gusto and found myself agreeing with him. We concentrated on our food and said little till we got back to the car. "Boy, I missed that diner almost as much as I missed you, Joan." We both laughed as he pulled away from the curb.

Twenty minutes later we were parked under a huge oak tree on Nanihagan Road. Al reached for me and I melted into his arms as if we had never been apart. He kissed me with all the pent up passion of our two year separation, and I responded.

"Oh, God," I heard him whisper in my ear. "How I missed you."

Then, without warning, he pushed me away from him and studied my face. "I love you, Joan and I want to marry you." He reached into his pocket and pulled out a tiny black box and handed it to me. I froze.

"Open it," he demanded.

I opened the box and there on a bed of black satin lay a diamond engagement ring. The diamond was tiny, but it sparkled in the afternoon sun. My mouth went dry and I was speechless.

"I know it's a small diamond, but I plan to trade it in on a bigger one," he said quickly. "I just wanted you to have something right now that tells everyone we are engaged. I bought it in Tokyo on "R&R" before we were shipped back home. Will you wear it, Joan? Will you agree to be engaged?"

I tried to speak but nothing came out. I just kept staring at the box.

"You do still love me, don't you? Please say you'll wear the ring."

He stared at me with pleading eyes. I finally found my voice and looked up at him.

"I don't know what to say, Al. I just didn't expect it. We haven't seen each other for two years. I thought we'd get reacquainted before we talked about anything else."

"I know I kinda sprung this on you, but I know you're the girl for me, and I guess I hoped you felt the same."

"I do, Al – I do. I just need a little time to get used to the idea of being engaged. And there's my family – I have to explain this to my mother and father. I'm sure they won't approve, especially my father. You know how protective he is. Just give me a little time, please."

"Okay, Joan. I'll give you two weeks. I'll keep the ring until then, so you can explain this to your family but then I'll want an answer. I've been thinking about you for two years, Joan. Please don't disappoint me now."

He pulled me to him again and kissed me long and hard. "You're the girl for me, Joan. I've made up my mind. Now, you have to make up yours."

He moved back in front of the wheel and started the engine. We drove back to my house in comparative silence. Thoughts were racing through my head. *How would I explain this to my mother and father? The idea seemed impossible. Engaged – me engaged?*

Chapter 11

"Engaged? But he just got back, Joan. Isn't this a bit sudden? What did you say?"

"That I had to talk to my parents and I needed a little more time."

"A little more time? You'll need a lot more time before we can get your father to accept an engagement. What can he be thinking? He doesn't even have a job yet."

"I know, Mommy, but he expects an answer in two weeks. What am I going to do? I love him but I'm not sure I'm ready to be engaged."

The phone rang. I looked at my mother and ran to answer it.

"Hi, it's me. How's my girl? What time can I pick you up tonight?"

"I can't go out tonight, Al. I have to be at work in the morning. We can go out on Friday."

"Friday? I have to wait until Friday to see you? I've been away two years, Joan. We've got some catching up to do."

"I'm sorry, but we'll have to do our catching up on the weekend. I have to get up at 6:30 to get the train to Manhattan and besides, my show is on tomorrow night."

"Your show? What do you mean your show? I thought you were a secretary."

"I am, but I also work on the *Richard Diamond* show on Tuesday nights. I hold the cue cards and prepare the promo."

"Well that's a hellava note. Now I have to compete with *Richard Diamond*?"

"I'm sorry, Al, but that's my job and I love it."

"You're supposed to love me," was the answer, and the phone went dead.

I put the receiver down and slumped to the floor. *He doesn't understand*. The tears began to come. I looked up to see my mother staring down at me.

"He's being so unfair, Mommy."

"He'll come around, Joan. He's been away a long time." My mother crouched down next to me and gathered me into her arms. "Don't cry, honey, you'll see him Friday night, and everything will be fine."

Friday arrived before I knew it. We were so busy at work that the time just flew and the *Richard Diamond show* with David Jansen went better than ever. We had the highest ratings for that time period of any network. The sponsor was so happy he threw a big luncheon for all the crew on the show. I was in my glory.

Al called around dinner time to confirm what time he was to pick me up. "We're meeting some of the guys at Pete's," he announced. "Can you be ready by eight o'clock?"

"Sure," I agreed. I waited for him to say he missed me but no words were forthcoming. "See you later," I said and hung up.

He was at the door by five minutes after eight – a record for Al Greene. A good sign, I thought. He didn't come in, just stood at the door till I returned with my jacket and purse. He walked ahead of me down the steps to the car and opened the door. I slid in. He hit the gas before my door was fully shut. The silence was deafening.

We got to Pete's in ten minutes flat and Al led me to a booth in the back of the bar. He ordered two beers and then turned to look at me intently.

"Have you thought about what I said? Did you talk to your parents about getting engaged?"

"I mentioned it to my mother, but she agreed with me that my father would never give his consent. It's too soon, Al. He needs time to get used to the idea of you and me going together again. Please try to understand."

"I'll give you one more week, Joan, -- one week, and then I want an answer." He downed his beer in one swig.

I could feel the tears welling up but I was determined not to cry. I sniffled and took a big gulp of my beer. I thought the evening would never end. I was so unhappy; I just wanted to go home. Al was busy playing catch-up with his buddies and didn't seem to even notice me.

After awhile he announced, "we're going to the diner for burgers, Joan. Don and Barb are gonna ride with us. C'mon let's get in the car." Before I even answered, Al paid the check and was pushing me out the door toward the car. I could smell more than beer on his breath so didn't want to argue. *After he gets some coffee in him he'll sober up.*

Three cars pulled away from the curb – ours squealing rubber louder than anyone. We made it to the diner in ten minutes flat. Al almost shoved me out of the car and up the steps into the diner. He was staggering a little, but I was sure the coffee would work a miracle. We crammed into a booth and ordered the usual – burgers with onions and coffee. After his second cup of coffee, Al seemed to be sobering up. It wasn't like him to drink the hard stuff. He was strictly a beer man, but some of his buddies must have decided he needed more of a welcome home so they bought him a few shots at Pete's.

I began to relax a little. He put his arm around me and whispered, "I'm sorry I acted like a jerk. It's just that I've been looking forward to seeing you for two years and then I had to wait till Friday night. A week's a long time, ya know."

"When you get a job, you'll have to get up early too," I said. "You won't want to go out till the weekend either."

"A job? Is that all you can think about? I've been working for two years in frickin' Korea. I think I deserve a rest, don't you?"

"Well, not if you keep talking about us getting engaged. You can wait awhile to look for work but let's stop talking about getting engaged until you do. At least then my father will listen. It's gonna take some time for you to find a job, Al. You know your mother can't support you and she's going to need financial help too. Your Army checks won't be coming in any more and your discharge pay isn't going to last forever. You don't even have a car. You have to be sensible. We're in no position to get engaged right now."

He looked me straight in the eye for the first time that evening. "You're right," he said. "I hate to admit it, but what you say makes sense. I'll start looking for work the first thing Monday morning and I won't mention getting engaged until I have a job. But then—look out, Joan, 'cause I'm not gonna take no for an answer."

Chapter 12

Al kept his promise. A few weeks went by but work still eluded him. Having had no college whatsoever, he had no skills to offer except his experience in construction. His only talent was drawing and there was not much of a market for that. There was quite a bit of building going on in the northern part of the county so he didn't seem too worried.

"Something will turn up," he insisted one Friday night. "I have an appointment with the foreman of a construction site up in White Plains on Monday morning. I have a good feeling about it."

His good feeling turned out to be a lucky omen. He got hired by a construction crew building ranch houses in a new development. With his innate ability to master electricity and plumbing, they were happy to get him. All was well and he was pulling down a pretty healthy paycheck every week.

"I hope you're putting some of that paycheck away," I suggested one evening.

"You sound like a wife already," Al declared, grinning. "I'm doing just that," he assured me. "After all, I'm gonna need a car. Can't keep borrowing Frank's all the time."

I smiled back. "I guess you're on the right track then."

The weeks and months flew by. Al still didn't like us getting together just on weekends but he wasn't going out that much during the week himself.

"I'm pretty beat when I get home from the job," he admitted one night at Pete's. "I see now why you insist on going to bed early during the week. Getting up at 5:30 a.m. is a killer. It's like being back in the Army. Staying home is helping me save money though. I'll have enough to put down on a car soon and then we can start thinking about getting en............."

"Whoa, Al. Not another word. We're not there yet. We both have to save money first. I just got a raise at ABC now that I'm permanently assigned to the *Richard Diamond* show, and I'm going to put as much of that away as I can. I hope Daddy doesn't raise my rent."

"You mean your father charges you rent – to live in your own house?"

"It's not my house, Al. It's his house and he never lets me forget it. Of course I pay rent. Don't you?"

"Well . . er. . . . no. No, I don't," he answered." I guess I should though – especially now that my Army checks don't come in any more. Mom started taking in borders to make up the difference and it didn't even occur to me to pay her board. Frank will be moving out soon now that he and Connie are getting engaged. He's doing real well at ABC. He's their top TV time salesman downtown at 30 Rockefeller Center. By the way, do you ever see him, Joan?"

"Since I'm way uptown at West 66th, we seldom run into each other. I did meet him at a Christmas party once when we were all at Tavern on the Green."

The memory of this unhappy occasion came to mind. Frank had made a scene at this party, reprimanding me for kissing one of the salesmen under the mistletoe.

"You're my brother's girl. You have no business kissing another guy," he had insisted, slurring his words after several glasses of champagne.

"I haven't seen your brother in over a year," I defended. "We have no serious understanding. I'm free to date anyone I choose and if I want to kiss Stan under the mistletoe that's my business." I stormed off, leaving Frank flushed with embarrassment. I never saw him again until we went to pick up Al at the airport a few short months ago.

Frank Greene was not one of my favorite people. We never really got along from the first time we met – like oil and water Al had said at the time. Nothing had happened to change that. It didn't help that we worked for the same company, but at least we were at totally different locations and seldom had to be in one another's company.

The very next week Al was quick to assure me that he was paying his mother rent. "She still does dressmaking for a living," he said, "but that just covers the taxes and the oil to heat that big house. Now that she has a boarder contributing to her income, I think she'll be all right but I am giving her money every week anyway. After all, I still eat at home most days and she has come to depend on me. Besides, it makes me feel better to know I'm helping her and the money I give her isn't paying for Frank's college. I really got upset when I found that out, Joan. I was sending the money home from the Army to help her pay her bills not to educate my big brother. After all, I never had a chance to go to college. Why should my money pay for him to go?"

"Did you ask your mother why she used the money for Frank?"

"Yeah. She said he couldn't get another student loan so she had to help, and my checks were just what she needed to do that. He's always been her favorite and I guess she wanted him to get a college degree. He always had big ideas of making lots of money and she thought college would help. At any rate, that's all in the past now. Frank is making enough money now that he can help Mom out financially too."

I seriously doubted the truth of that statement, but refrained from commenting.

Two months later Al announced he had a surprise for me.

"You'll find out what it is on Friday when I pick you up," he announced, excitement evident in his voice. "No clues till then."

When the doorbell rang on Friday night I hurried to the door. Al was standing there grinning from ear to ear. "C'mon Joan, let's go. I can't wait to show you the surprise."

He took my hand and all but dragged me down the steps to the curb. "There," he said. "Isn't she beautiful?"

I was dumbfounded as I took in the sight before me. A shiny navy blue Ford convertible gleamed at the curb. As I walked around the back of the car, I was in for another shock -- it had a rumble seat.

"Wow," was all I could manage.

"Do you like it?" he asked anxiously.

"Like it? Of course I like it. It's gorgeous – and a rumble seat too! I've never even sat in a rumble seat. It's so shiny. You must have spent hours polishing it."

"Well, it did take awhile to get it to shine like that," he admitted sheepishly." I really wanted it to dazzle you, Joan, and by the look on your face, I think I succeeded. Get in and let's take her for a spin."

He opened the front door with a flourish and I climbed in. The seats were soft leather and the dashboard was trimmed to look like wood. It was so sporty, and I must admit I was impressed. I sat back in the seat and prepared to enjoy the ride.

Chapter 13

The new car led to a new job and a bank account for Al Greene. The months flew by. Before I knew it we were singing Auld Lang Syne and welcoming in 1953. Talk of engagement was in the air again and finally things came to a head.

"Either we get engaged or it's all over," Al announced one evening. "I want to go down to the City where Frank suggested and put a deposit on a ring, and I want to go on Saturday."

He paused, waiting for me to say something. I was dumbfounded but finally found my voice.

"I'm having a wisdom tooth pulled on Saturday. Did you forget you were going to take me to Dr. Hudson?"

"Of course not, but that's the beauty of it. We'll already be in the city so why not make a day of it. The diamond district isn't far from the dentist and we can go right there after you have your tooth pulled."

"But I'll have anesthesia, Al. I may be sick or knocked out. I won't be in any shape to go ring shopping. This is an important decision; can't it wait for another day?"

"No, it can't, Joan. You've put me off long enough. It's Saturday or never. I mean it."

"Okay, Al. We'll go on Saturday." I knew better than to argue any further.

The big day arrived. When Al picked me up Frank and Connie were with him.

"They're gonna pick out Connie's ring today too, Joan. The Greene boys are gonna do this together. Isn't that great?"

"But what about the dentist, Al? I asked anxiously.

"Not to worry. They're gonna do some shopping while you're at the dentist," Al informed me. "We'll meet them at the jeweler's in the afternoon."

"I sure hope I'll be up to it," I said.

The surgery had been a nightmare. Dr. Hudson almost had to put his foot on my chest to get enough leverage to extract the stubborn wisdom tooth. I bled like a stuffed pig and he had to give me more medication than he planned. On top of the pain, I was so swollen on the left side of my face I looked like a lopsided blow fish. I could hardly open my mouth and the pain was excruciating.

Needless to say, when Al came to pick me up I was a sorry sight and in no mood for a romantic trip to the jewelry store. However, his enthusiasm was paramount right now and my physical state took a backseat to his plans. He offered a few perfunctory comments about the way I looked but did not overwhelm me with his compassion. That should have been a clue to our future but I hurt too much to think about it.

"I guess you don't feel much like eating right now, Joan," he questioned.

"No," I mumbled, holding the side of my face. "Let's just get this over with so I can go home."

"Okay, hon. We'll just head down to the jewelry store and meet up with Frank and Connie."

Al helped me into the car and we drove off without another word. As we approached the store I saw Frank and Connie standing out front. Frank spotted us and waved Al over to the curb.

"I saved you a spot in back -- in the alley," he said and pointed behind the building.

"In the alley? You want me to park my car in an alley? Are you nuts?"

"This is New York City, Al," Frank quipped. "Where the heck do you think you are going to park? My car is there too. Stop being such a worry wart. Park the car and stop complaining."

Al grumbled loudly but finally shrugged and got back in the car. "You wait here with Frank and Connie, Joan. I'll park and be right back."

I got out and walked over to my future in-laws and waited.

"Wow," what happened to you?" Connie asked.

I explained and she just shook her head in disbelief.

"I'm so sorry, Joan. I had no idea what you were having done. From the way Frank talked, I thought it was a routine checkup. Men…ugh."

"Thanks, Connie, but I'll be all right once the swelling goes down. Al just didn't want to wait another day and there was no use arguing. He had made up his mind."

"Sounds familiar," Connie said with a grin. "These Greene boys are tough to handle some times. C'mon let's go inside and wait for Al. Might as well start looking at rings now that they've got us here."

She took my arm and led me toward the door. Al was already coming around the corner, grumbling under his breath about his car. We ignored him and all went inside together.

Connie and I seemed to have the same taste but I had Al's budget uppermost in my mind. Frank had told her to pick out whatever she wanted. Al had given me no such guidelines. I led him away and wandered from counter to counter until I felt a bit more comfortable with the size of the stones mounted in the rings laid out below me.

"These stones are so small," Al said. "Let's go back up where Frank and Connie are."

"We can't afford those rings," I said sternly. "The ones they're looking at are at least a carat and maybe more. I don't want you to go into debt for my engagement ring. You just started working and you haven't been able to save much yet. The payments are gonna be pretty steep, ya know."

Al looked at me and lowered his head. "I know I don't have a big job like my brother, but I want you to have a ring you like and will be proud to wear," he said. "I don't want your father to think I don't care enough to buy you an expensive ring."

"The heck with my father. I don't need an expensive ring to make me happy. Just let me pick out something I like that you can afford, okay?"

"Okay," he answered grudgingly, "but let's move up to the next counter at least. I see some pretty nice rings in that one."

I followed his gaze and walked to the next counter. I looked down at the dazzling display in front of me and suddenly I knew.

"That one," I said, pointing to a half carat blue white diamond in a square gold setting.

Al stood beside me and looked down where I was pointing.

"I like it too," he said quietly. "Let's ask the jeweler to let you try it on."

He walked over to where the jeweler was talking to Frank and Connie. "Would you let us see a ring down here, please?"

"Of course, sir," he replied and strode to the counter where I was standing. "Which ring would you like to see?"

I pointed to the one I admired. He unlocked the case and brought out the ring, placing it carefully on a velvet cloth on top of the glass counter.

"Feel free to try it on," he said.

I slipped the ring on my finger and held it away from me. The stone sparkled and I loved the way it shimmered in the light. I looked at Al. He was transfixed. The jeweler stood by quietly.

"What to you think, Al?"

"I think it looks great, but, do you like it? You have to like it. That's the main thing."

"I do, Al. I love it. It's a bit more than I think we can afford but I really love it."

"That settles it then."

He looked up at the jeweler and with all the authority he could muster he announced, "we'll take it. Can I pay for it on time?"

"You've made an excellent choice, sir, and I'm happy to inform you that your selection is on sale this week at ten percent off. There's no problem paying for it on time. You just have to sign a contract to that effect."

"Wow," was Al's response. "Guess it was meant to be, huh Joan?"

"Will the young lady be wearing the ring, sir, or do you want a box?"

"A box," I interrupted.

Al looked at me quizzically but said nothing till the jeweler disappeared into the back of the shop with the ring. He returned momentarily with a tiny black velvet box and a document for Al to sign.

"How much will you be putting down today, sir," the jeweler inquired.

Al hesitated, looked at me and then drew his checkbook out of his pocket.

"How about a hundred dollars down?" he said.

"That will be fine," said the jeweler and the monthly payments will be spread out over two years in the amount stated in the contract. If that is satisfactory, just sign here."

Al looked at me again. I nodded and he signed the document and made out the check. In a matter of minutes we were done. I could hardly believe it. I was so exited I had almost forgotten about my swollen face and aching tooth. After all, I was engaged to the man I loved.

Al rushed over to Frank to tell him the good news. They had settled on a ring also and were preparing to finalize the deal. Connie was all smiles and I knew she had found the ring of her dreams too.

"What a day," I said as I hugged her. "We got engaged family-style."

She grinned and hugged me back. "We'll both be Mrs. Greene before long I guess."

Chapter 14

I couldn't wear my engagement ring at home. Every day on the train coming home from work, I would take it off and put it in my purse. I told my mother about the ring the day after we bought it. Although she appeared happy for me, she begged me not to tell my father just yet.

"He's not ready for that, Joan. Please wait a few months till I can soften him up."

Al was not happy with this idea but agreed to go along for awhile. His acquiescence lasted till February of 1954 and then he exploded.

"I want to be officially engaged," he announced one Saturday afternoon. "We've pussy footed around your father long enough. Frank and Connie have been engaged for months now and have already set their wedding date, and here we are still keeping it a secret. Enough already!" he shouted. "And besides that, I want to set a wedding date -- in May." He paused, waiting to see my reaction.

"A wedding date too? How much do you think he can handle at one time? We didn't even talk about that. Why May?"

"Because it will be your birthday. We might as well give it to him all at once. You want to get married, don't you?"

"Well, of course I do. I just didn't think we would do it so soon."

"So soon? We've been unofficially engaged for almost a year now and we talked about a spring wedding. Well, spring is around the corner so now is the time."

I begged him to let me talk to my mother first but to no avail.

"Either you tell him tonight or I will."

"All right. I'll tell him tonight at dinner and we can face him together when you pick me up at eight."

"Agreed," was his only response.

I couldn't wait until dinner. When I got home, Daddy was ensconced in his favorite chair with the newspaper strewn around him. I walked up and stood by his chair, facing him. He looked up.

"I'm getting engaged to Al Greene and there's nothing you can say to change my mind. I have a ring and I intend to wear it. We're getting married in May and you're invited if you care to be there. If you don't, we'll get married anyway."

I stopped speaking and tried to breathe. Daddy was red in the face but said nothing. I waited a minute and then turned to leave the room.

"Just a moment, young lady," boomed the voice from the chair. "Did you say engaged? I don't recall your asking my permission."

"I didn't and I'm not asking it now, Daddy. I'm telling you. I will be twenty one years old this May, and I can get married if I want to. You said you've been putting my rent money away to pay for my wedding and now is the time to get it out. We just want a small wedding in church and a simple reception at the Women's Club so it won't cost too much. I hope you'll be happy for me but if not, having my mother and brother there, will be enough. Al's family is happy for us so they will be there to wish us well too. I hope you'll decide to come."

I turned and left the room and didn't look back. I bumped straight into my mother as I was rushing around the corner to the stairs. I wanted to get to the safety of my room as quickly as possible.

"What happened, Joan? Is the devil himself after you?"

She pulled me into the stairwell.

"No, Mommy. I told Daddy I was getting engaged and also getting married in ……..''

"Married?" she interrupted. When did you decide that?

"We just decided today. First I thought on my birthday but then I changed my mind since that is a holiday. So we picked the twenty second 'cause it falls on a Saturday. Please don't be angry. Al is right. We've waited long enough. I'll be twenty one and old enough to make up my own mind."

"You're right of course, Joan. I understand and you have my support. After I get your father calmed down can we sit down and talk about the details of this new plan. If I am to be the mother of the bride, I have some planning to do, and there's not a lot of time left either."

"Oh thank you for being so understanding, Mommy. We'll sit down tomorrow and talk about it all you want. Right now I want to calm down and get ready for my date with Al."

"What about dinner?"

"I'm too excited to eat right now. I'll get something later."

I ran upstairs, leaving my poor mother to unruffle the feathers of my angry father in the living room.

When Al knocked on the door that evening my heart sank. I opened the door and literally pulled him inside.

"I told him," I said. "I even told him we'd be getting married in May and he could come if he wanted to."

"If he wants to? That's what you told him? Boy, you don't mince words do you? But I'm proud of you, Joan. Really I am. Do you want me to talk to him?"

"Not unless he asks you to." I mumbled hopefully.

"Al Greene, is that you?" boomed the voice from the living room. "I want to talk to you."

Al looked at me briefly and then strode into the living room.

"You want to see me, sir?"

"You bet I do. What is this crap about you marrying my daughter?"

"It's the truth, Mr. Carney. We're engaged and we've set the wedding date for May."

"So my wife informs me," he retorted. "Doesn't anyone ask me anymore?"

"No sir, not this time. We know how you feel about us getting married, so we just took matters into our own hands. And now, if you'll excuse me, your daughter is waiting for me to take her out on the town. We have something to celebrate."

Mommy and I were floored. We couldn't believe that Al would stand up to my father like that. I was so proud of him I wanted to applaud. Needless to say, I didn't push our luck. I grabbed my jacket and was waiting for Al at the front door. We fairly danced down the steps.

Chapter 15

The next few months were like something out of a movie. My father vacillated from a knife-wielding drunk threatening to kill Al Greene if he ever looked at his daughter again to a typical draconian male parent making wild promises if I would comply with his wishes. Nothing made any difference. Al and I never wavered in our path to the altar. The wedding plans progressed nicely under the management of my dear mother, and father was not consulted about any of the pertinent details.

One of the hardest decisions I had to make concerned my maid of honor. The Church insisted that this attendant be a Catholic and all my friends, including my dearest one from grade school, Carol Crockett, were all Protestant. What a dilemma. Al's cousin, Virginia, was Catholic but only in her teens so I had to choose Kay, my friend from work and the only Catholic girl friend I had. She agreed to be my maid of honor and Carol and Virginia were bridesmaids.

Al was a bit upset about our not being allowed on the altar in my parish in New York. Frank and Connie were recently married in New Jersey and that state allowed them to go on the altar and he could not understand what prevented us. He also did not want to sign the paper agreeing to bring our children up Catholic. This would have been my breaking point and we actually suspended our engagement for a few weeks while he sulked over this point. I would not give an inch and when he finally realized it was hopeless to argue further, he gave in, albeit angrily.

The day loomed sunny and seemingly calm. My father was also fairly calm as he labored under the influence of several Phenobarbital prescribed by the doctor. When it came time to leave for the church he took my arm and led me out the front door of our house. As soon as we hit the third step down to our walkway across the lawn it began to rain. A sun shower lasted just long enough to wilt my recently coifed hair and leave water spots on my white satin shoes. An omen, I wondered?

Daddy had parked his big Buick at the curb in readiness to receive the bride in her gown and train. My mother helped stuff me into the back seat and got into the front next to Daddy. He turned the key. The engine made a strange grinding sound but did not turn over. Daddy swore and turned off the key. He tried again. This time he swore louder and told my mother to call our neighbors and see if we could borrow their car. She hopped dutifully out of the car and just as she hit the curb, the neighbors were backing out of their driveway. Mommy ran out in the road and waved her arms. They stopped. She must have explained our dilemma because Mr. Smith came over to the car and handed Daddy his car keys.

"Here you are, Charles. Use our car to take Joan to the church. Ann and I will call a cab."

My father stammered his thanks and got out of our car. He helped me out of the back seat and we walked over to the Smith's car where my mother was waiting to stuff me into the front seat next to my father. I almost disappeared under the train of my dress which she had to fold into piles in my lap. The car was a Ford coupe with a very small back seat. My little five foot mother barely squeezed into the back. My father turned the key and the motor hummed amicably. We drove to the church arriving only about five minutes before the ceremony. Daddy was still cursing under his breath as we pulled into the parking lot. I noticed that Al's car was already there. This was probably the only time in our relationship that he was ever on time – and early to boot.

As we hurried up the steps of St. Eugene's Church I saw him peering out of the door with an anxious look on his face. Frank was grabbing his arm and turning him around. It wouldn't due for him to see the bride before the ceremony. My mother rushed me into the bride's room where I found my loyal bridesmaids waiting anxiously for my arrival. I explained briefly what happened and we set about distributing floral bouquets and doing last minute checks of their nylons and cleavage.

"We're ready for you, Joan," said my mother. "I'm going to take my seat now. Daddy is in the foyer waiting to walk you down the aisle."

"Okay," I said. "We're all ready in here. Break a leg, girls," I said to my bridesmaids as they headed out the door to make their trip down the aisle.

As I stepped through the door, Daddy took my arm and positioned me at the end of the aisle. My Aunt Rose spread my train out behind me and blew me a kiss. The organ began the strains of The Wedding March and I took my first step on the arm of my father. I turned to look at him. His face was passive but stern. I whispered, "I love you, Daddy." He looked straight ahead but I felt him squeeze my hand as we started down the aisle.

After what seemed like hours I found myself mechanically shaking hands with a mile-long line of well wishers, accepting kisses and hugs and then magically, I was running down the stairs of the church under a canopy of rice with my new husband by my side.

I remember almost nothing of the ceremony – it all seems a blur. We had to stop in the park for pictures before going on to the reception. My father was having words with the photographer when we arrived. It seems he called him "Pops" and this sent my father into orbit. Nobody calls him "Pops" – not even me.

After what seemed like a hundred photo shots we were back in the car and heading for the reception at the Bronxville Women's Club. There was no sit-down dinner planned – just hot and cold hors d'oeuvres and lots of champagne. My father had informed me in no uncertain terms that this was all we could afford, based on my accumulated rent. The food was excellent and the champagne wasn't bad either, so everyone had a good time.

By the time we cut the wedding cake and passed it out to all the guests it was almost five o'clock. We left our guests and changed into our "going away" uniforms. My last act of the evening was to throw the bouquet and my bridesmaid, Kay, was the ecstatic recipient. We left for our honeymoon night in Manhattan with cans clanging from our rear bumper and a huge "Just Married" sign plastered on the trunk. We were driving to Miami Beach for our honeymoon but would spend our first night of wedded bliss at the Drake Hotel on Park Avenue in New York City.

The deed was finally done. I was Mrs. Al Greene and this was the beginning of our life together. I never thought we'd make it.

Chapter 16

The wedding night was uneventful and the biggest disappointment of my life. We had splurged despite our meager finances and booked ourselves a room at the famous Drake Hotel on Park Avenue in Manhattan. The cost for this huge extravagance was a whopping $19.95 for the night which even included a glass of champagne for the bride and groom. We really thought we were special and it felt wonderful until it came time for the main event.

What was all the hullabaloo about the earth moving and fireworks? I was bursting with youthful passion and though my groom appeared to be too, his priority seemed to be speed. I had heard the expression "wham, bam, thank you Maam," but never dreamed it would be applicable to my honeymoon. Dreadfully disappointed – I found it painful, uncomfortable and more of a nuisance than anything else. Where had all the tenderness gone – all the building up to the close calls on Nanihagan Road? I assured myself it would get better. After all, I had made him wait for quite a while to consummate our love.

We left for Miami Beach in the morning after a trip to St Patrick's Cathedral. It had been a dream of mine to attend Sunday morning mass there. It took us almost three days to get to Miami and so we spent two nights on the road in motels. I was sure the situation would improve. After all, this was my honeymoon. It didn't get any better and by the time we arrived in Miami Beach there was no doubt in my mind – I was definitely frigid. I had read about this in magazines – women who couldn't feel passion and who went through life "faking it." If this was to be my fate, I would have to work at the art. I determined not to think about it any more and to concentrate on enjoying our time together in Miami Beach.

The first day was very cloudy but we lay out on the sand to rest after the long drive. Al and I both fell asleep and when we woke up, he was burnt to a crisp. Because there was no sun out, we hadn't bothered to put on any suntan lotion, and now we were paying the price. Al took his shower first and when he came out I could not believe my eyes. His insteps were swollen almost two inches. They were puffed so high, he could barely walk and could not get his shoes on either foot. He put on a pair of slippers and we headed for the car. We drove into town and went to the first drugstore we could find. The druggist took one look at Al's feet and declared, "sun poisoning."

"Put this cream on right away and stay out of the sun," he warned. "Keep some cream on all the time. It will take a week or so to heal. You've got to watch those cloudy days," he added. "They are treacherous."

Al looked at me and shrugged. We returned to The Neptune Inn on Collins Avenue, to consider our next course of action. We perused the guide books and picked out a few places we wanted to see. We would have a good time without going to the beach if it killed us. And we did. We visited all of the local attractions and found some wonderful restaurants too. I was relaxed, because Al was in such pain that we had to avail ourselves of the twin beds in our room each night. This took the pressure off to "perform" and the week sped by in an amicable chain of events. The maid gave us a strange look every morning, but we didn't care.

By week's end Al was feeling better and we were able to head north. We had found an apartment on Marlborough Road in Yonkers. It was a tiny third floor unit in a private house on a pretty tree-lined street with a set of stairs straight up from the front porch to our front door. The rent was $85 a month but we thought we could swing it if we were a bit frugal. I was still working at ABC and Al was in construction but looking for something more stable and less physical.

"I don't want to be chained to a desk," he would remind me. I'd go nuts, but I don't want to work outside all my life either. A dilemma we agreed, but for someone with no specific skills, it wasn't easy to get a decent paying job. I could hear my father's voice in my head, "He'll never amount to anything with no college education." This was not an option for us, however, as we barely made enough money between us to pay our bills and put a tiny bit away.

One day there was an ad in the paper for a silk screen artist in a local studio. Al answered the ad and was granted an interview. He knew nothing about silk screening but was willing to learn, and he could draw, so he decided to give it a shot. He got the job and started work a week later. His hours were 8:00 a.m. to 4:00 p.m. so it wasn't long before he was bugging me to quit my job in the city and get one locally. I was still doing the *Richard Diamond* show which got me home at 10:30 p.m. one night a week and the other nights I never got home before six.

"We 'd be saving all the money it costs for you to commute and you'd be home early so we could have dinner together. I hate eating so late or by myself when you're working late. C'mon, honey, give it some thought."

He kept up this campaign until I finally gave in. Reluctantly, I quit my job at ABC and went to work in an insurance agency in Bronxville as secretary to the owner and president. He was a wonderful boss and eventually I learned to overlook the boredom of the insurance industry and found pleasure in meeting and working with nice people. The commute was only fifteen minutes by car so that was a bonus too.

Not long after I joined Rollins Insurance Agency I found myself pregnant. Mr. Rollins was most understanding and told me I could work as long as I wanted to. He nicknamed me the pink flash as I made so many mad dashes to the ladies room in the months that followed. I had morning sickness for nine full months and lost 30 pounds. We couldn't afford maternity clothes so Al donated one of his pink shirts (thus the nickname.) to my wardrobe. My mother, God bless her, made me several outfits and treated me to a few things from the local maternity store.

Before leaving Rollins to have my first baby, I introduced Al to the representative from the Royal Globe Insurance Company who offered him a job as an insurance adjuster. The only catch was he had to go to college, but the company would help pay his tuition. Much to my amazement, Al agreed and enrolled in night school at Columbia University in the Bronx. He quit his silk screen job and began working as an insurance adjuster for Royal Globe in the New Rochelle area. He used our car to make his calls but got mileage on an expense account so it was not a hardship. He loved the job because he was not tied to a desk and could make his own schedule to get the job done. Things were looking up.

I gave birth to my daughter, Elyse, three weeks late on December 27, 1955. Although Al always said he wanted a son, he adored our daughter from the moment he laid eyes on her. He selected her name and would not discuss changing it. To this day I don't know where he got it from. They were buddies from the first time he held her in his arms. Sometimes I even felt a little pang of jealousy when I watched them together. I still thought I was frigid but I worked hard to conceal it.

We stayed in our tiny apartment for three years until I became pregnant again. We had been trying for quite awhile and had just about given up. The doctor told me I would probably never have any more kids based on the fact that it took me a year to conceive the first. When we proved him wrong, Al was thrilled. Now he would have his son. His brother, Frank, already had two sons so, of course, our second child had to be a boy.

We were getting real tired of having Elyse's crib in our room. She had been climbing out of the crib since she was a year old so sleeping even a little bit late on a Saturday morning was out of the question. She was everywhere at once in the tiny apartment and we were all getting a bit stir crazy. We started house hunting in earnest.

In a moment of weakness my father had offered to loan us the money to put down on a house if we needed it. So, when we found a little house in Mount Kisco, we were thrilled. One of Daddy's engineers had just bought one in the same development and my father had commended him for his fine choice. We were sure he would be pleased with our selection and would be thrilled to provide us with the loan he had promised.

"You want to buy a house in that crummy area? Are you out of your mind? Those houses aren't worth the money to burn them to hell."

We were speechless when we heard his answer. The houses were good enough for his engineer, but not for us? Al lost it! His temper flared and he told my astonished father where he could put his money and how he could get it there. I was shocked, but secretly was cheering as my husband put my arrogant father in his place. He never gave us a penny, but strangely enough, his attitude toward Al changed from that day forward. I think his outburst gained my father's respect -- not an easy task.

Our lack of funds forced me to concede when Al begged me to agree to buy his mother's house for a "token fee" and allow her to live with us. She assured us that she would not interfere with our lives and that we could renovate the 100-year old house any way we wanted. Living on the "wrong side of the tracks" in the snobby town of Bronxville and with a built-in mother-in-law to boot was not my idea of heaven, but the school was considered first class and that was a big consideration for Elyse's education. Al's mother and I had gotten along famously up to now so why should living together change it?

It was a big house – six bedrooms and a huge dining room with a fireplace all contained in three full floors and a basement. It had a small yard and the Bronx River ran behind the house. I knew it would take a lot of work but neither of us was afraid of hard work, and so we embarked on the adventure.

Chapter 17

In the spring we moved into the big house on Parkway Road. Al's mother insisted we take the big front bedroom on the second floor complete with an alcove big enough to hold a crib, a small dresser and a bath and changing table. Our furniture fit in nicely and I made a draw drape to close off the alcove where the baby would be in early November. We began our renovations with the kitchen which had no cabinets whatever and extended our plans to the adjacent butler's pantry which we converted into a laundry room and small powder room. These changes were our priority and we worked hard to complete them before the next baby was born.

The morning sickness never left me with this pregnancy either, so that should have given me a clue. November came and went and still no baby. I was so tired of answering the phone, "Yes, I'm still here." Finally on Sunday morning, November 30th I made a decision. I left a note for Al, who had gone to the lumber yard and packed my bag.

I walked the four blocks from our house to the hospital with my tiny suitcase and declared to the admissions clerk that I was checking in.

"I am staying here until this baby decides to be born," I insisted. "She was due November 4th and here it is November 30th and she is still not ready. Who ever heard of a ten-month baby?" I wailed.

The nurse smiled and assured me I could stay. She called the doctor and explained why I was there. He agreed to the admission and said he'd be around that evening to check on me. Dr. Allison, our family doctor, was true to his word and arrived right after the dinner tray had been removed. He checked me over and announced that I was not yet in labor – something I already knew quite well. He patted my rather large stomach and said he'd be back in the morning.

Labor started about 4:00 a.m. and by 10:00 a.m. I was ready for some kind of pain relief. I had given birth to Elyse with sodium pentothal which was painless, but I didn't feel like I was part of the experience because I remembered nothing about it. I had told Dr. Allison that I wanted to use natural child birth this time, using only a mild muscle relaxer. He had agreed, but when the labor pains were coming hard and fast, the nurse could not find him to give me the muscle relaxer. Apparently, he was in the cafeteria having coffee. By the time they located him I was fully dilated and ready to give birth. There was no time for any medication.

Alison (with one L) was finally born at 11:00 a.m. on December 1st. She was 6 lbs. 2 oz. and 19-1/2 inches long. All I could think of when I looked down at her was, "O my God – another girl. Al will kill me." This time I picked the name and filled out the form before Al ever got to the hospital to see her. I had always wanted an Alison and now I had one. She was the most beautiful baby, and I was overjoyed.

Al arrived an hour or so after she was born. He seemed disappointed but tried to reassure me. "The next one will be a boy for sure," he insisted. When he came back from the nursery after seeing his second daughter, he was smiling despite himself. "She sure is a beauty," he said. I smiled in agreement as he leaned down and kissed me. "Another December baby," I whispered.

And so, life returned to normal. Elyse had her own room next to ours and we kept Alison in the alcove with us. Being four years older than her baby sister, Elyse was a big help to me. She loved helping with her baby sister and when Ali looked up at her, it was love at first sight.

There was never a hint of jealousy. All went well for the first three months until I began to feel sick again. I went to Dr. Allison and could not believe his pronouncement. "You are pregnant again, my dear."

The words hit me like a slap in the face. I went home and looked down at my sleeping three-month old and could not believe I was pregnant again. The tears stung my eyes. I couldn't help it. I remember the feeling as if it were yesterday. We could not afford another baby. I couldn't go back to work and Al wasn't making that much money at the Royal. There was hope for a raise soon, but we couldn't count on it just yet. And then there was the house. We still had the living room and dining room to do and Al was talking about moving a wall to open up the hall and putting in a new I-beam. All this took money, and if I was pregnant, how would I be able to help him with two kids to care for?

Al's brother, Frank, and our old neighbor from Marlborough Road pitched in, and before I knew it the wall was down, the I-beam was up and we were tearing wall paper off the walls in the living room in preparation for painting. We had to finish the living room in time for Christmas because the new baby, like his or her siblings, would be born in December. We had our hearts set on a live Christmas tree to sit in the big bay window and so we worked harder than ever and got it done before I had to leave for the hospital.

Beth was due on December 10th but waited until the 13th to be born. This time Al took me to the hospital and after Dr. Allison delivered her, my husband announced she would be called Betty Lou, the name of his old girlfriend. I always thought this was in retaliation for my producing another daughter. I objected of course, but he informed me he had already filled out the papers. I was furious. As soon as he left I called the nurse and demanded the papers back. I think I scared her into submission. She brought them the first thing in the morning and I changed her name to Elizabeth Jean. I wanted to call her Emma but my mother pleaded with me not to, as she had always disliked her name. So, I used my dear mother's middle name and chose Elizabeth, knowing we would call her Beth.

The nurse told me later that I cried uncontrollably when the doctor announced it was another girl. I was convinced that my husband would be furious and would never forgive me for giving him another daughter. I was wrong, of course, although once again I could see the disappointment in his eyes. *Why don't men understand that we are not responsible for the sex of our offspring?* Beth was tiny too, weighing in at 6 lbs. 1 oz. like her big sister Elyse. Funny, I always thought I'd weigh a ton and have huge babies. Instead I lost 30 lbs. with each one and they were all small.

I didn't know what busy was until I had two babies, a year apart. It was like having twins. I didn't know who to attend to first. Thank God for Elyse; she was my saving grace. My mother-in-law helped some but my other savior came in the body of her mother who came to live with us too when Beth was about a year old. *Two mother-in-laws and four generations of women under one roof—what a scenario.*

Great Grandma was a blessing in disguise. The girls just gravitated to her and she could keep Elyse and Ali busy for hours while I tended to Beth. We quickly finished another bedroom on the third floor and moved Elyse and Ali into it. We realized we would have to move to the third floor ourselves pretty soon as the stairs were becoming too much for Al's mother. When Beth was six months old we bought bunk beds for the girls' room and put her in with her two sisters. Al and I took the small front bedroom and gave his mother back the big master suite so she could use the alcove as her sewing room. Her mother now resided in what had been her sewing room on the second floor, so this worked out well. Al's mom was still working as a seamstress and needed a place to set up shop. We still had one bedroom left on the 3rd floor which we planned to give to Elyse as she was the eldest.

Fate took a hand once again and no sooner did we move Beth in with her sisters than I was pregnant again. This time I was due in November instead of December but with only 18 months between births. *How could this be happening to me?*

To make matters worse, my dear mother was once more in the hospital battling her old nemesis, cancer. She was not expected to make it this time and here I was pregnant once again and with three kids at home to care for. I needed to be at the hospital each evening with my father who was not taking his wifely abandonment well. My husband stepped up to the plate and, with the help of his mother, settled the kids down every night so I could be at my mother's side. I prayed that she would survive long enough to witness the birth of my son – this time it would be a boy; I was certain of that, and I wanted her to know.

It was a very difficult time as my father did not handle it well. He was more concerned with himself and who was going to take care of him than he was with my mother's illness. He loved her in his own way and, although he knew she was suffering, he was unable to concentrate on anything but himself. I learned to hate him during this time.

Chapter 18

I never had morning sickness even once after I found out I was pregnant. This fact convinced me it was a boy. I was even more certain when I developed bronchial pneumonia at the end of August and was taken to the hospital in an ambulance. I coughed so hard I ruptured the cord and almost coughed my baby loose. The doctor on call informed me I had undoubtedly killed the baby by delivering more than two months premature. He got out the red pen and began drawing on my belly, preparing me for a Caesarean Section. That's when I knew for sure that it was a boy. I rose up on my elbows and looked the doctor straight in the eye.

"Forget the pen. I will have this baby normally. I've had all my babies normally and I will not have a Caesarean now."

"It is impossible for you to go into labor at this stage, Mrs. Greene," the doctor said adamantly.

"You watch me," I shouted and laid back down on the gurney. I prayed like I have never prayed in my life. They moved me into a small labor room and, in between racking coughs; I managed to go into labor two hours later. As usual, my God had not abandoned me. Al had gone back home after assuring me he would return as soon as they would let him.

The labor was hard but short and the outcome was a 3 lb 1 oz. baby boy. Al, Jr. burst into the world on September 2nd which was Labor Day that year. Talk about irony! I finally had my son, and I was thrilled. Though tiny and weak, he had all his vital parts and was breathing on his own almost immediately. He was placed in an incubator and it was 72 hours before I was allowed to hold him in my arms.

Although I agreed to name him after his father, I did not want two Als in the house. My mother had struggled with two Charleses all our lives and I vowed I would not go through what she did. So the nurses and I got together to think of a nickname that did not represent any other name. After much deliberation, we came up with Brett. Although he was legally Al, he was called Brett all his life until many years later when he went into the Navy.

Al was thrilled to finally have a son and I could not wait to tell my mother. My father had called to tell me she was getting worse each day and was on so much morphine that she barely knew he was there.

"When are you coming to see her?" was all he could say.

"As soon as I am released, Daddy; I promise, was my constant answer."

I had to remain in the hospital for a week to be sure the pneumonia was totally cleared up but Brett had to stay until he achieved 5 lbs. I had Al take pictures of him through the glass window at the hospital so I could take them to my mother. As soon as I was released Al took me to see her. We brought the slide projector and showed her pictures of her grandson on the wall of her hospital room. Although severely medicated, she was still aware enough to know that she had a grandson. I silently thanked God for giving her that gift before we lost her.

We brought Brett home three weeks later and kept him in a bassinette in our room until the last bedroom on the third floor was complete. Our little boy improved steadily under the watchful eyes of his three sisters, two grandmothers and his parents. He never wanted for attention and my only regret was that I could not bring him to the hospital so my mother could see him. I tried to persuade the powers that be, but it was no use. So I spent my days caring for my son and my nights sitting at my mother's bedside watching her deteriorate.

It took my dear, sweet mother twenty six weeks to pass on, and it was agony watching her die a little more each day. On November 26th my father and I were at her bedside as usual. She was in a morphine induced sleep at this point so was not communicating, but somehow I knew that she was aware of our presence.

"I want to go home now, Joan. I'm exhausted," whined my father.

"Not yet, Daddy; I have a feeling we should stay a little longer."

"We've been here since six o'clock and it's almost eight thirty. Please take me home," he insisted. "I need to get some rest, and Emma is not going to wake up again."

I pleaded with him to reconsider, but it was no use. When he made up his mind there was no changing it. I finally acquiesced and we headed for the parking lot. I was angry and we didn't speak a word to each other all the way home. I pulled in the driveway and we went in through the garage and up the cellar stairs. Before we entered the kitchen and I turned on the light the phone started ringing. I ran to answer it.

"Mr. Carney? Your wife passed away just a moment ago."

I glanced at the kitchen clock. Five after nine the hands showed –twenty five minutes since we left the hospital, twenty five minutes more we should have stayed and been there to say goodbye. I muttered thank you, hung up the phone and burst into tears.

"What happened, Joan? Who was on the phone?" my father asked.

"The hospital," I sobbed. "She's gone. She died right after we left. You couldn't wait another half an hour. It's all your fault we weren't there to say goodbye. I'll never forgive you for that, never."

I rushed to the front door and slammed it shut behind me. I had to get away from him before I said something else I'd be sorry for. I wanted to get home and be alone with my thoughts.

Al looked at my face and knew what had happened the minute I walked in the door. He came toward me and held me close.

"I'm so sorry, Joan, so very sorry. Come sit down and tell me what happened."

He listened to my story in between sobs and attempted to comfort me.

"He's just a selfish old man, Joan, and we have to feel sorry for him."

"I hate him, I hate him," was all I could muster.

The next week was a nightmare. My father left everything to me – the funeral arrangements, the casket selection, the wake, the church services – everything. He was like a helpless child whose only concern was what would happen to him now. It turned my stomach. My brother, Charles, was my support system. He had it worse than I did as he was still living at home with our father, but he tried to help me with the decisions as much as possible.

I walked into the funeral parlor the first day of the viewing to see how they had prepared my mother. When I entered the room where the casket was awaiting transfer into the viewing room, I almost had a heart attack. I looked down on the face of my once beautiful mother who now weighed barely eighty pounds and saw nothing but the bright red mouth. They had used the brightest, reddest lipstick I had ever seen on her mouth and it made her look like an emaciated harlot. I was appalled! I grabbed a tissue from the side table and began wiping off the lipstick as my tears fell onto her face. The man who stood with me was horrified at my actions and tried to stop me. I almost hit him but my brother convinced him to back off. He watched in silent horror as I re-colored the rouged mouth with a soft pick shade I had in my purse. My brother patted my shoulder, then took my hand and led me from the room.

Somehow we got through the next few days. To be honest, a lot of it remains a blur. My poor brother found himself waiting on my father hand and foot. Even his girl friend, Bunny, pitched in and cooked meals for the two men. No matter what she prepared, my father complained. I knew Chuck would not be able to stand it for too long, and I was right. A week later he and Bunny announced their engagement and the wedding was planned for a few months hence. Before he knew what hit him, my father was living alone in the big house on Seneca Avenue.

Daddy was furious. "You have all abandoned me," he said. "No one ever cared about me but your sainted mother. You'll regret this, mark my words."

And so we did, when six months later he married a woman from his office that we had never heard of, much less met.

"I can't be alone. I need someone to take care of me," he shouted when I questioned his decision to remarry before a year had passed.

I went to his priest for comfort and found none. "After all, Joan, he's sixty one now so why do you care?" was his explanation "He doesn't want to be alone that's all. It's no insult to your mother. Get used to it."

And so he married Florence and prepared to sell the house. Al and I made him a reasonable offer but he turned us down. He ended up selling it for less than we offered. Why was I surprised? He never did intend to help us financially no matter what lies he told us in front of my mother. The newlyweds moved to a condo in Ardsley.

Before he closed on the sale of the house on Seneca Avenue, I asked my father if I could have something from the house of my mother's. He assured me that Florence would leave something in the garage for me to pick up the following day. When we opened the garage door, I saw that there was a package on a chair in the corner. I unwrapped the plastic grocery bag and saw two single bed sheets. I opened the first sheet and saw that it had been patched in the center – something my mother was prone to do, being so careful in how she spent my father's hard earned money. The second one was a duplicate of the first.

I burst into tears remembering how he had called me the day of her funeral and had me come and get everything of hers – clothes and jewelry and shoes. At his command I ransacked her closet and dresser drawers and threw everything into her set of luggage and brought it home. I no sooner walked into the house than the phone was ringing.

"This is your father speaking. I want you to bring back the luggage and all your mother's jewelry tomorrow, first thing. You can dispose of the clothes, but I want the jewelry – all of it. And by the way, that includes the pearl ring she gave you in the hospital."

I was rendered speechless. *What kind of man was this?* "I will return everything you asked for but not the pearl ring. She gave me that herself in the hospital. She wanted me to have it. It's all I have of her and I will not give it to you." I hung up the phone.

I silently prayed that I would never have to speak to my father again as long as I lived.

Chapter 19

Weeks and months passed without any communication between my father and me. I was so busy at home taking care of my four children and helping my husband re-do our 100-year old house that I simply put him out of my mind. My brother and I kept in touch and Al and I would visit Chuck and Bunny in their new apartment in Yonkers at least once a month.

The phone rang one evening, and when I picked it up and heard my father's voice on the other end, I had to steel myself not to hang up.

"I'm moving to Florida," the voice said. "I bought a condo in Boca Raton and we're leaving next month."

"Oh," was all I could muster.

"I'll mail you the address and phone number when we get settled."

"Fine," I said. "Have a good trip."

"Thank you and give my regards to the children."

The phone went dead. I turned my back and walked into the kitchen. Alison was sitting at the table attempting to feed Brett his lunch.

"Pop Pop sends you his love," I said. "He's moving to Florida."

They looked at me wonderingly but no one answered. He was not a part of their world. My father was never a big part of our lives so his absence had little or no impact. Al and I kept working hard on the old house and finally finished it by the time Beth was ready for Kindergarten. The floor plan had changed too. Both grandmas were now on the second floor with Alison and Beth sharing the middle room outfitted with bunk beds. Elyse finally had a room of her own on the third floor with Al and me in the front and Brett in the tiny bedroom at the rear. I remember well that it took me one whole week to clean that house from top to bottom. By the time I got to the end of the third floor hall, it was time to go back down and start in the kitchen again.

The dining room was my pride and joy. It had two huge windows – floor to ceiling—on each end and a fireplace surrounded by blue delft tiles on the back wall. Al had built in corner cupboards on each side of one window and made a chandelier out of a huge wagon wheel for the center of the eleven foot ceiling. We refinished the oak floors and furnished the room with an old antique oak pedestal table which shone from its many coats of wax. Six matching chairs picked up at auction completed the setting. We purchased a wonderful hutch for the wall opposite the fireplace and Al found an old oak chest of his father's to sit under the window near the kitchen to complete the décor. It was a beautiful room conducive to happy family dining.

We didn't have much money in those days and what we did have went into the renovations and furnishings of the house. We did, however, have a nice group of friends and so gave dinner parties once a month. I loved to show off this beautiful room when it was my turn to be hostess. My mother had taught me how to sew and utilize the new drip-dry sheets that were so popular then. Beautiful flower patterns were available and they made lovely fodder for floor length hostess skirts which were the current rage.

Grandma Julia had taught me how to cook Hungarian stuffed cabbage and some of the other culinary nuances of her native country so my friends were always anxious to share our international cuisine. It was good fun and those were good years.

Elyse was in need of braces now and. although Al was doing pretty well at the Royal, we did not have enough money to cover this large expense. I begged Al to let me go back to work and finally he relented. I got a job at Lord & Taylor selling gifts and linens on Thursday nights and all day Saturday. I didn't make much but it helped put the braces in our daughter's mouth. I loved the job and made friends with many of the ladies I worked with. The store was frequented by several well know celebrities as many of them lived in Westchester County where we were located. During my sales career I waited on the likes of Richard Widmark, Theresa Brewer and Jack Parr to name a few. As a matter of fact, I picked out all the towels and sheets for Mr. Widmark's bath and boudoir. He was single at the time and at a complete loss as to what to buy for his new home in the Westchester hills.

About this time Al and I decided we wanted to take a family vacation. As always, money was an object. The solution was to allow me to work more hours to help pay for a few weeks at the beach in Cape Cod. Our dearest friends had moved there the year before and we missed them a lot. We visited them briefly once and fell in love with the Cape. I figured out that if I worked from nine to two every day so I could be home when the kids got out of school, and all day Saturday, I could make enough to pay for our vacation. I suggested this to Al and after a bit of cajoling and wifely persuasion I convinced him. How else could we get a vacation with four kids? He finally agreed and we booked ourselves a cottage on the beach in Sandwich, MA, the first town on Cape Cod.

Lord & Taylor was very good to me and transferred me from gifts to the elegant Salon. I made a bit more money there working with the expensive designer ensembles, and even did some in-store modeling; and then my big chance came. I made friends with Miss Caroe, the head of the Interior Design Dept. She needed an assistant and when the time came, she chose me. I was thrilled not only because of the raise in pay but for a chance to prove myself and have a real career. She agreed to teach me everything she knew. I took to the job like a duck to water and couldn't wait to get to work every day. I made enough to pay off Elyse's braces and now I was able to pay for our vacation. I was feeling very proud of myself.

Our first two summers at the Cape were wonderful, but then things began to change. Little by little I began to realize that things were not so wonderful at home. While we were at the Cape with our friends, all was well but when we returned to Westchester our marriage was not what it should be. My first clue was the houseguest forced upon me the next summer. She was the sixteen year old daughter of Al's old girl friend, Betty Lou. We had visited Betty Lou and her husband at their home in Bermuda in the spring that year and met her daughter. Before I knew what hit me I heard my husband say, "We'd love to have Wanda come with us to the Cape."

The first week with Wanda was a nightmare for me and the kids. She hung onto Al like he was her big brother or worse – her boy friend. The girls couldn't get near him most of the time because Wanda was always there, fawning over him, and he was eating it up. I held my tongue until one day when I found Elyse crying.

"Daddy loves Wanda more than he does me," she whimpered. "Us too," chimed in her two younger siblings. I tried to allay their fears and managed to succeed to some degree until the final insult. I awoke the next morning rather early and rolled over in the bed toward my husband when I heard an intake of breath. I looked up to see Wanda peering over the bedroom wall staring down at us. The cottage had a natural peak with no ceiling – just eight foot partitions separating the various rooms. The little trollop had climbed up on a piece of furniture in order to attain this position so she could watch us in bed.

I was enraged. I woke Al up and told him to get that Jezebel out of my house. Even he was shocked at her behavior and told her so – in front of his newly awakened daughters too I might add. He was due to return to work that week and was planning to leave on Monday. We had planned to keep Wanda for another week and then send her home with Al when his vacation was over.

It was now Sunday which meant she could leave with him tomorrow. Thank God. She was not too upset by the idea of leaving a week early as she could drive home with the object of her affections. I for one didn't give a damn as long as he got her out of my sight and away from our kids. I helped her pack in relative silence and was happy to bid them both farewell the next day.

I had a whole week to think about what had happened and wonder how a grown man could permit such behavior in our home – even if she was the daughter of an old friend. The more I thought about it, the more I decided it was just a case of male ego. Wanda was attractive and very mature for a sixteen year old and Al was only a man after all. I did wonder about the phone calls he got from Betty Lou periodically though. That had been going on for about a year I knew.

I chose not to waste any more time on the subject and concentrated on enjoying the remaining week of our vacation. Al came back of course, but we didn't talk much about it. He laughingly accused me of being jealous. He dismissed it as the mischief of a silly misguided teenager and that was that. I wondered if he was right but decided to put it out of my mind altogether. Life went back to relative normalcy.

Chapter 20

After our return from the Cape, life continued without incident in the Bronxville house and soon the girls forgot the unpleasantness of the prior summer. Elyse had her father's undivided attention once again and when the next summer arrived, we began enjoying long lazy days at Jones Beach on Long Island. The kids loved it and even Brett managed to get some of his father's attention – a rare treat for our little boy. We had to plan our trips for Sundays as I still worked at Lord & Taylor every Saturday, a big day for interior design business.

One evening Al announced that Judy, a secretary at his office, would be joining us on our Sunday trip to the beach. I was a bit annoyed that I had not been consulted but didn't see any reason to make an issue of it. He told the kids to call her Aunt Judy, which rather surprised me as she was barely out of her teens herself. We picked her up on the way to Long Island and headed for the beach. We found a great spot on the sand not too far from the water and settled in. The girls headed for the water immediately, dragging their father and Aunt Judy with them. I stayed behind and played with Brett making sandcastles on the shore.

After a while the girls came out dripping and shouting. I noticed that Al and Judy headed up the beach at a brisk walk. "Daddy says he needs some exercise," said Alison. Aunt Judy wanted some too so she went with him."

"They didn't ask me to come," said Elyse. "Daddy and I always take a walk on the beach to look for shells."

I detected a tear rolling down her cheek amid the salt water drops on her face so I suggested we all go back to the blanket and have a snack. That suggestion met with applause and we walked up the beach.

I broke out the soda and some chips and everyone dug in. Al and Judy did not return for over an hour. By the time they sauntered up to the blanket I was furious. I was determined not to lose my temper in front of the kids but I was seething. I offered them something to eat and then moved away toward the water. Brett toddled after me and I scooped him up and went into the surf. I managed to work off my anger fighting off the waves with my tiny son in my arms.

The rest of the afternoon passed without incident but I avoided my husband's eyes and made no effort to add to the conversation on the trip home.

Several weeks later, I heard from the kids that Aunt Judy had once again accompanied them to the beach, but on a Saturday this time while I was working at Lord & Taylor. I lost it. This was not appropriate fatherly behavior in my book. When Al came home that night I let him have it.

"What the hell is going on with you and Judy?" I demanded.

"Nothing," he stammered. "Why do you ask?"

"The kids told me you took her to the beach again while I was working."

"Yeah, so what?" was the reply. "Poor kid had nothing to do that day so I offered to take her. What's wrong with that?"

"Everything!" I countered. "She's not a poor kid; she's a young woman working in your office who should be spending time with guys her own age, not a married man with four kids."

"You're just jealous," he shouted.

"I guess I have reason to be." I retorted, especially since this is not the first time."

"What do you mean by that?"

"Your kids keep me well informed, Al. I heard about the others too. Judy isn't the first secretary you've taken pity on and invited to join you at the beach when I was conveniently at work. I'm telling you right now, it has to stop. I'll put up with a lot but I've reached my limit on this. I suspected that you were unfaithful but now I'm certain of it, so I'm telling you I will not put up with it. If you behave in any way that touches me or the kids adversely, I will leave you. I swear to you I will."

"Very funny," was the reply. "And where do you think you'll go? You've got nothing of your own and I'll see to it that you never get the kids. You'll never leave me so stop threatening."

Things went from bad to worse after that. I asked Al to leave our bedroom but he refused. I didn't want to make a scene with his mother and grandmother living in the house too so I swallowed my pride and spent the next year or so clinging to my side of the bed. Sex was never an issue any more, thank God, unless he got drunk and then it became nothing more than a rape which I learned to tolerate in silence. Our marriage became a sham but I worked hard at putting up a front for the kids and my two mother-in-laws. Al did not make waves so we survived in an atmosphere of congenial apathy.

Later that year something happened that changed all our lives. The village of Bronxville opened a skating rink down the hill behind our house. This was an activity we could all do together as a family regardless of how Al and I felt about each other. One afternoon Al and I were sitting on a bench having a cigarette when another couple strode over to do the same. Almost at once, I recognized the man. He was of average height, a bit stocky and had piercing brown eyes. His most memorable feature was his wonderful wide grin and soft deep voice. I remembered him in school plays and being the one who made everyone laugh. We didn't run in the same crowd and had never dated in high school but he was one of those guys that everyone knew and liked.

"Pat?" I asked. "Pat Foley from high school?"

He looked at me for minute and then grinned. "Joan? Carney isn't it?"

I nodded. "It's me," I said. "Boy, what a small world."

"This is my husband, Al Greene."

Al stood up and the two men shook hands.

"Pat was two years ahead of me at Roosevelt," I offered. We haven't seen each other for quite a few years.

"And this is my wife, Jean," Pat said. A tall, slender, brunette walked over shyly and introduced herself. Jean was rather quiet, but we all seemed to hit if off. Even the kids got together and began exchanging addresses and phone numbers. What seemed like an accidental encounter became one of the most important events of all our lives.

Chapter 21

The months that followed became some of the happiest in my life. Jean and I became best friends and Al and Pat got along famously. They were both adept at telling jokes and could keep us all in stitches for hours. When we were out in a group with other friends all you had to do was provide a category and they would start telling stories, competing with one another for the best punch line. Our kids got along too and the girls saw a lot of each other after school. We were like one big happy family.

Strangely, when the four of us would go out for an evening, Pat and I would sit together as would Al and Jean also. Anyone not knowing us would think that Pat and I were married to each other and so were Al and Jean. In retrospect, it was not really strange at all. The Foley's marriage was in about the same shape as ours. Jean knew full well that there was no love lost between Al and me, and admitted the situation was the same at her house. We both admitted we would have left our husbands if it wasn't for the kids. This new liaison was keeping both our marriages together.

This went on for months. We hung out in a wonderful German Brauhaus in Armonk where the bar tender became a friend and confidante.

I don't know if he ever caught on that we were not what we seemed. He assumed that Pat and I were together as were Al and Jean and we never bothered to correct him. We laughed, talked, danced and drank huge quantities of beer. As time went on I noticed Jean was drinking more and more beer. Many nights we got her home just before she passed out.

Pat called us one night about 2:00 a.m. Al was in no mood to get up and go out so I got dressed and went to their house. Jean was barely conscious on the bed with a bottle of vodka half empty next to her. I rushed to her side and held her close, like a child.

"Oh, Joan, she mumbled between sobs, I'm so sorry. I'm so unhappy. I just can't live like this ...." Her words trailed off and I felt her slump in my arms.

"She's gonna have to sleep it off, Pat. I'll put her to bed and come over again first thing in the morning." I tucked her in, turned off the light and went downstairs.

Pat was waiting in the den. "Thanks so much for coming over. I just didn't know what to do with her. She's been drinking a lot lately. I even found another bottle of vodka hidden in the back of her closet. Something is eating at her to make her drink like this. I hope she'll tell you 'cause she sure won't tell me."

"I'll see you in the morning," I answered sleepily, "and I'll try talking to her tomorrow."

The next day I went to see Jean. Pat had left for work and she was alone in the kitchen staring into a cup of coffee.

"Thanks for taking care of me last night. Pat was pretty mad at me and I guess I don't blame him. I can't go on like this, Joan. I've got to get outa here. We just can't stand being in the same house together. It's awful."

I tried to soothe her but it seemed useless. Finally, in frustration, I stood up and announced I was leaving. "I'll call you later," I said. She nodded and I went out the back door to the car.

I called Jean later in the afternoon but there was no answer. I figure she went out to do some shopping – that always cheered her up. I called again after Al and I finished dinner and Pat answered.

"She's gone," he said. "I just got home from work and found a note on the mantle. She packed some clothes and left for Florida.

"Why Florida?" I asked.

"I have no idea," Pat said "except that she does have an old girl friend down there. I'll try and find her phone number and see if she knows anything. I don't know what to tell the kids, Joan. What can I do?"

"I don't know what to say, Pat. She didn't say a thing to me. I wonder if Al knows anything. Let me talk to him and I'll call you back."

Al was watching TV in the living room. I walked in and stood by his chair. He looked up.

"Did you know Jean was going to Florida?" I asked.

"Florida? What are you talking about?"

"I just called her. Pat answered and told me she had packed some clothes and left for Florida. She left a note but didn't say why she left or where in Florida she was going. We thought she might have said something to you. Did she?"

"No, she didn't say a word to me, but I'll tell you one thing. I'm gonna fly down there and bring her home."

I was dumbfounded. "You're what?"

"I'm going to bring her back," he answered.

"Why you? She's Pat's wife."

"He doesn't love her," Al responded. "He doesn't care if she's gone."

"And you do?" I asked incredulous at his attitude.

He didn't answer. He turned on his heel and headed for the stairs. Before I could say another word he was gone. I heard the bedroom door slam on the third floor. My first thought was to call Pat and relay this unusual reaction. I picked up the phone and heard my husband's voice on the line. I put my hand over the mouthpiece and listened. He was booking a flight to Ft. Lauderdale, FL. I put the receiver down—gently. *So, he did know. She must have told him.*

I waited in the living room till I heard him come down stairs. The kids were all in the basement playing so we were alone.

"Why did you lie to me? She's my friend too."

"I didn't lie. Jean talked about doing this for some time but I didn't think she meant now."

"She must have been awfully unhappy." I suggested.

"Yes, she is," he answered. That's why she's been drinking so much lately. She and Pat are not getting along at all. I guess she just couldn't take it any more. So, I'm going to bring her home and I don't want to talk any more about it."

With that, he walked over and turned on the TV.

"Aren't you even going to talk to Pat about this? It's his wife, after all."

"No," said Al. "I'm just going to fly down to Florida and bring her home."

"How do you know she'll come?" I asked.

"Oh, she'll come alright. Don't you worry about that. Now stop asking me questions. This will all be over soon enough. I'll have her home before the weekend."

I was speechless. I couldn't think of another thing to say. I heard my mother-in-law in the second floor hall and decided to let it go. I didn't want her to get in on the act. She certainly wouldn't understand any more than I did and she would surely pester her son with questions which would only infuriate him and they would end up in a row. Last time that happened, Al put his fist through the wall in a rage. His mother had an art for driving him to distraction as she always had to have the last word.

It was time to get the kids ready for bed but I did want to call Pat first and let him know what was going on. He was as shocked as I was but decided to go along with Al's plan and see what came of it.

Just as I hung up the phone, Brett came up the basement stairs looking rather sleepy.

"Elyse helped me with my homework, Mom. I'm going up to my room now."

"Okay, honey. You use the bathroom first and then I'll call your sisters. Our nighttime ritual had begun. I put Jean out of my mind and went to attend to my children.

Chapter 22

Al did exactly what he said he'd do. He flew to Florida the next day and brought Jean home. He walked in our front door looking like a storm cloud.

"She's home," he said. "We'll go over there tomorrow morning right after breakfast and get this all straightened out."

"Okay," was all I could think of to say.

Next morning I made our usual Saturday banquet of pancakes and sausages and we all ate together in the kitchen.

"What are we gonna do today?" asked Alison.

"Yeah, what?" Beth joined in.

"You're all gonna stay here and play. Elyse will be in charge till Mommy and I get back," said Al with authority.

"But where are you going?" came a chorus of voices.

"We have to go to Aunt Jean's," I said. "She needs our help with something," I offered, grasping at straws.

"Why can't we go too and play with their kids?" asked Alison.

"Because I said so," answered Al. "Now, no more questions. Grandma is upstairs but don't bother her unless it's an emergency. We'll be home soon."

"You guys do the dishes for me, okay?" I shouted as I headed out the door after my husband.

We drove to the Foleys in silence and when we pulled into the driveway, Pat came out on the porch.

"C'mon in. I just made another pot of coffee," he said.

We entered the kitchen. Jean was seated on a stool blowing into a huge mug of coffee.

"It's too damn hot," she muttered.

"Hi," I said and ran over to give her a hug. As I held her, she put down the mug and began to cry, holding onto me all the time.

"Please forgive me," she moaned. "I didn't mean for this to happen. I'm so sorry.........so sorry." The tears kept coming and I stepped back to look at her. She appeared totally distraught and making no sense whatever.

"Just tell me what's wrong, Jean. You're my best friend. I'll understand."

"Noooooooooooooo you won't she sobbed. You won't ever forgive me."

Both men kept silent through this dialogue. I glanced up at Pat, hoping for some help. He looked away. Al was staring out the window and was offering no help either. I forged ahead.

"Jean, I can't help you if you don't tell me what's wrong."

Jean wiped her eyes with the back of her hand and got off the stool. She cleared her throat.

"I'm in love with someone else; that's what wrong," she blurted out. I have been for awhile. I didn't know what to do about it so I ran away. Al came and got me and here we all are."

The silence was deafening. I felt my legs shaking under me and forced myself to sit down. Pat still said nothing and Al was pacing at the back of the room.

Pat finally broke the silence. Jean and I are splitting up," he said. "We talked it over this morning and she's going to stay in the house with the kids and I will move out into an apartment. I'll support her and the kids just the way I always have till we can get a divorce. It'll be fine. We've been unhappy together for a long time now. It's just as well that it finally came to a head."

Al stopped pacing. "If there's anything we can do to help, you have only to ask. I hope you know that," he said. He looked at me and I nodded in ascent.

"I guess you know Joan is going into the hospital in two weeks for a hysterectomy and then after one week at home, we'll go to the Cape for a month so she can recover. It'll be a lot easier for her there and the kids can kinda take care of themselves. I know you planned to rent a cottage up there yourselves but I guess you won't do that now."

"It's too late to cancel," said Pat. "I already paid the fee for our three weeks. Jean and I will have to decide what to do. The kids are really looking forward to their vacation."

"Well, whatever you decide, you know we'll be there for you." I said. "We'll leave you now and head on home. I'm sure you've got a lot to talk about--- and with the kids too."

I walked over to Jean and gave her a hug. She hugged me back but looked so forlorn I could hardly stand it. I hated to see her so unhappy.

I wonder if she remembers that I am planning to leave Al after I recover from the hysterectomy. I told her about his latest affair with his current secretary and that I had vowed that I would not put up with any more of his infidelity, and this time there would be consequences. I guess she's too preoccupied with her own problems right now. I wonder who the man is. She hinted that there was someone else but she never told me who.

A phone call had come in the middle of the night a few months back that forced me to make the decision to leave. Al's then-secretary had called, crying hysterically, "I'm pregnant," she announced, "and he won't acknowledge it. He won't help support me, and wants nothing to do with me," she wailed. You must talk to him."

Her pregnancy? He had gone too far this time. Not only would he take no responsibility for what he had done, but he was actually going to pretend it never happened. I was speechless with anger and humiliation and, in utter desperation, I hung up the phone.

What kind of man had I married? He wasn't just a philanderer. He had no scruples.

There was no way I could continue to live with this man. I had to get away, despite the cost to me and my children. My choice had been made for me. I called Jean that night and told her of my decision. She said very little, but let me get it all off my chest. She was very sympathetic, but didn't encourage my anger. She even agreed to let me store some of my clothes at her house so I would have less to move when the time came. I assured her I would do nothing until I was fully recovered from my surgery and she seemed to understand.

We never spoke of that call again although I did bring several boxes of clothes over to her house the following week, and she stored them in the basement for me.

Chapter 23

⧚∾

Pat and Jean made a decision. Jean and the kids would go to the Cape as planned. Pat would come up on weekends. Al assured Pat that he would watch over Jean and the kids in his absence and help out whenever he was needed.

Meanwhile, I had a successful hysterectomy and had two weeks to recuperate at home before going to the Cape for our month's vacation. The two families would be together one last time and I would use the time to get my strength back. I was still determined to leave Al in mid September as soon as I had my final checkup. I had put this decision off long enough. I had received several more incriminating phone calls from his secretary regarding her pregnancy, and that was the straw that broke the camel's back, as they say. I had warned him that if he ever brought disgrace to our family I would leave him. I know he didn't believe me, and would never vacate the house, especially with his mother in residence also. As hard as it would be to leave the kids, I could no longer live like this. He had left me with no dignity whatever and I had to make myself a strong drink just to have the courage to open the door and face him every evening when he came home from work. This was not the way I wanted to spend my life.

The warm sun and peacefulness of the Cape was like a balm to my soul and I was able to recover more quickly than I had hoped. I even managed to take our tiny sailboat out onto the lake one day all by myself. It was sheer joy, skimming along with only nature for company. The kids were a big help to me and, although I didn't see too much of Jean, knowing she was there if I needed her was a comfort. Al looked in on her every day and our kids played together as they always had. The days went by easily and without any undue stress, for which I was exceedingly grateful. Pat came up only one weekend and spent a lot of time with his kids, fishing and swimming and riding bikes. They were thrilled to have him all to themselves for a few days.

As soon as we returned to Bronxville at the end of August, I went to the yellow pages and looked up a local lawyer. I found one in Tuckahoe, a nearby village, and made an appointment. I learned that in New York State there were only three ways you could get a divorce – desertion, adultery or a one-year legal separation. Since Al was not about to desert me and proving adultery, which was his obvious crime, would be a long and ugly business (especially with four kids) I opted for the legal separation. The cost was $85 which was something I could afford and so I proceeded with that course of action. The lawyer was a kindly old gentleman, one year from retirement, who encouraged me to get what was due me from my eighteen years of marriage. I explained my situation as I perceived it, including the few assets we owned as a couple. Our second meeting was an eye-opener.

"Joan, I am sorry to inform you that your home is in the name of your husband and your mother-in-law which means you have no claim to it whatever. The few shares of AT&T stock you had bought from your brother have been sold. The only asset you hold jointly is a lot in Cape Cod. The car is also in your name. Other than that, you will get nothing from this marriage. I strongly suggest that we include in the separation agreement a stipulation covering a monthly gas and maintenance allowance for the car as well as a small stipend for your personal use."

I was terrified by this information. I was impoverished except for half the cost of a lot worth $4000 and a six year old station wagon. I had nowhere to go and no form of income. I knew I would have to leave the kids in the house till I could find a place for us, but now even that seemed impossible. I signed the papers and determined that I would leave in two weeks. I called my brother, told him of my plans, and asked if I could stay with him for awhile till I found a job and a place to live. He agreed, of course. The next thing was to explain the situation to the kids.

They were all back in school now that Labor Day was past. I waited for the weekend and took them aside one by one to explain what would happen the next weekend. Elyse was sixteen now so understood pretty well, but was very angry. *How could anyone leave her absolutely wonderful father?* Twelve year old Alison sobbed until I assured her we would be together as soon as I found us a place to live and that I would see her as much as I could. Beth, at eleven, was the pragmatic one.

"Leave him a note, Mommy, she instructed. "If you don't, he might go to Lord & Taylor and get you fired. I'll give it to him after you leave. I'll hide your suitcase on the porch so Daddy won't see it."

Brett was another story. Being only nine and the only male in the house beside his father who paid little or no attention to him, preservation was uppermost in his mind. "Can you give me a quarter, Mom?" he asked. I almost cried as I handed him two coins from my purse.

On Friday, September 15th, the night before my intended departure, I called my brother to alert him that I would arrive --bag and baggage the next day. My pronouncement met with a brief silence. "What's wrong?" I asked. "Isn't it still okay for me to come?"

"You won't believe this, Joan, but our friends from Australia are in town and want to stay with us this weekend. It's the only time they can visit us and Bunny and I didn't know what to say. Please forgive me. They'll be gone by Monday morning and then you can stay as long as you like. Can you put it off till Monday?"

Now it was my turn to be silent. Thoughts ran wildly through my head. I made a decision.

"No, Chuck, I can't put it off any more. I've already told the kids. I'll call Pat. Maybe I can stay with his mother. We are dear friends and I'm sure she won't mind. Please don't worry about me. I'll call you Sunday night. I love you."

I hung up the phone and called Pat who was now in his own apartment in Eastchester.

"Of course you can go to Mom's," he soothed. "She'll be thrilled. You know how much she loves you. I'll call her right now and call you back."

In fifteen minutes my plans were made. I drove to Pat's with two suitcases full of my belongings and asked him to hold them for me until Monday when I would go to my brother's. I had taken the day off at Lord & Taylor and I agreed to be at his house by ten o'clock so we could drive to his mothers. I would leave my car in Eastchester and pick it up again on Monday.

When I returned home, I wrote a note to Al which I gave to Beth in a sealed envelope and hid my small overnight bag on the porch behind one of the chairs. Elyse was in her room and I went in to say goodnight. She barely brushed my cheek with her lips and let me hug her only briefly. I tucked in the three younger ones and spent my last night on the couch in the living room.

On September 16th I left the house on Parkway Road for the last time as a tenant. I fingered my rosary as I drove to Pat's apartment and prayed that my children would forgive me and that maybe a new and happier life awaited me.

Chapter 24

I had a wonderful weekend with Pat's mother, despite my unhappiness at leaving my children. She managed to make me aware of the good that would come out of my decision and to assure me that my kids would forgive me eventually – even Elyse. Pat stayed with me too and we took long walks in the adjacent woods and watched the sun set every evening. I began to relax and soon the glass appeared half full rather than half empty.

My brother called Sunday night to assure me that I would have a bed waiting on Monday. I called the kids to let them know where I would be and that I would call them again soon. Sleep came more easily that night.

The next morning Pat drove me to my car in Eastchester and then he caught the train into Manhattan. I drove up to Connecticut to my brother's home to begin my new life as a single mother. My sister-in-law did everything possible to make me feel at home in their charming little house at the edge of Six Mile River in Darien. The house dated back to 1785 and had once been a country store at the bottom of the street on which it now stood. It had only two small bedrooms on the second floor and I was to occupy one of them. Chuck and Bunny had no children.

After trying every medical avenue open to them for the past fourteen years, they had finally given up and accepted what they thought was God's will. So now Bunny had someone to "mother" and she gloried in it. Though I missed my children dreadfully, I felt loved and wanted and part of a family. I will always be grateful to them for giving me this respite in the midst of my storm.

I took a week to settle in, calling my kids each night to tell them I loved them, and then began to look for work in earnest. I started with an employment agency in White Plains, NY, only a half hour commute down the Merritt Parkway. I had not worked in an office for fifteen years. So, even though I had the prestige of being a Katharine Gibbs graduate and had worked for the last nine years at Lord & Taylor; my secretarial skills were a bit rusty. I had not taken shorthand in all those years except for notes on a grocery list or brief instructions from my boss, the decorator. My eyes had never encountered an electric typewriter, which was the elite office machine in use these days.

The morning I walked into the employment agency dressed in my only business suit, I was a nervous wreck. I filled out all the forms and survived the personal interview. Then it was time to take the typing test. That was a disaster! The interviewer grinned as she sat across from me with the test in her hand.

"You are a charming and smart young woman," she said, "but this is the worst typing test I have ever seen."

She held up the sheet of paper. There were long strings of a's at the beginning of many of the lines interspersed with multitudes of apostrophe's on the other end. I lowered my eyes. She waited.

"I must admit I have never seen, much less used, an electric typewriter before," I offered.

"Didn't you type at Lord & Taylor working as an assistant decorator?"

"Yes," I answered sheepishly, "but the typewriter is an old manual Royal. You need a touch like a longshoreman to make the keys go down."

"Oh," she laughed. "That explains those a's and apostrophe's. You're nervous and these keyboards respond to a delicate touch. Each time you hit one of those keys at the end of the line you pressed so hard you got multiple impressions."

"I know I can do better," I interrupted. "I typed 120 words a minute at Katie Gibbs. I just need to get used to these new modern machines. Please give me a chance."

"Tell you what," she answered. "I have an employment request from a new Japanese firm here in town. You probably won't get much call for your shorthand skills but you will have to convince them you can type. You're a bright lady. I am confident that you'll be able to do that. I also have a spot open at Pepsi Corporate Headquarters so I'll get you appointments for tomorrow at both places and see how it goes."

I could have hugged her. "Thank you so much," I stammered. I promise I'll make you proud."

"I'll call you at home this afternoon and give you all the information you'll need for tomorrow. Good luck, Joan, and let me know how the interviews go. Remember, there is no cost to you; the company pays our commission, so just relax and do your best."

I fairly skipped to the parking lot and headed home to share my good news with Bunny. The phone rang about a half hour after I got in. Bunny handed me the phone.

"It's the agency," she said.

"Joan Greene," I said into the mouthpiece.

"This is Louise Long from the Wilson Agency. Here is the info on your two appointments for tomorrow. Hitachi is in the morning and Pepsi in the afternoon. Good luck and keep me posted."

"I will," I assured her, "and thanks for all your help."

I was so excited and I wanted to share my happiness with my kids so I called the Bronxville house.

"Hello." A serious female voice came over the phone.

"Hi, Elyse, it's Mom." The line seemed to go dead. "Elyse, are you there? It's Mommy. Please talk to me."

"Hi, Mommy. It's me, Ali. I miss you. When can I see you?"

"Hi, Ali. What happened to Elyse?"

"Oh, she handed the phone to me and went upstairs," was the answer. "But I'm here and Beth and Brett are in the kitchen doing homework. Are you coming over?"

"No, sweetheart, I can't come just now but maybe on Saturday. We could go to that park you like or take a ride or something. Let Beth and Brett know too, will ya? I just wanted to tell you all that I have a job interview in White Plains so I'll be working soon, but I hope to see you most weekends. Okay? Tell Elyse I love her too, and I miss you all so much."

"We miss you too, Mommy. I can't wait till Saturday. I love you."

"I love you too, Ali. I'll call you again before Saturday, I promise."

I hung up the phone and the tears started to come. Bunny stuck her head in the door and, seeing my face; she sat down on the bed next to me and put her arms around me.

"It'll get better, Joan, really it will and one day soon you'll have your kids with you. It won't be easy but it will happen. You have to believe that."

"Thanks, Bunny," I mumbled. "I think I'll just rest here awhile till Chuck gets home. See you later." She hugged me gently and left me alone. I closed my eyes and was soon transported to a kinder, gentler place.

Chapter 25

"This calls for a celebration," said my brother when he came home that evening and I told him my good news. "Let's break out a bottle of that Spanish wine we've been saving."

We drank to my good fortune and then I excused myself to go call Pat to let him know my good news too. He'd been my best friend and a pillar of support through this entire ordeal. He and Chuck had become real good friends too and he was always welcome in their home. He wished me luck and said he'd be up on the weekend to visit.

Before I reached the stairs to return to the living room, I heard an insistent banging on the front door. Bunny was in the kitchen so Chuck went to answer it. As I touched the bottom step I saw Al push his way through the door and knock my brother to the floor. I screamed. It startled him but did not deter him. He began hitting Chuck in the head with his fists. I screamed, "Bunny, call the Police."

This seemed to get his attention and he backed off for just a moment – just long enough for my brother to drag himself upright to a standing position. As Bunny rushed into the room, Al struck him again and knocked him across the room into an étagère loaded with picture frames and memorabilia which came crashing to the floor. Chuck's lip was bleeding and he looked dazed. Being three inches shorter than my ex was problematic but now he was so angry that he lost all reason and started swinging. He connected to Al's jaw with a lucky upper cut and down he went, bringing the coffee table with him. Just then the sound of a car in the driveway made us all pause. The black and white screeched to a halt and a policeman took the three front steps in one leap. He strode into the room and without a word separated the two men who were both hunkered on the floor at this point. Bunny was crying and I was in shocked into silence.

"Who wants to explain this?" the officer asked, looking first at Al and then at Chuck.

"This S.O.B. is keeping my wife," Al muttered, slurring his words.

"I'm her brother, you damn fool," countered Chuck. "She left you. Don't you get that?"

The cop looked from one to the other and then at Bunny and me. I stood up.

"He's right, officer. That man is my husband and I left him a week ago. I have filed for a legal separation. I am staying with my brother and his wife until I can get a place of my own. Apparently my husband has been drinking and decided to pay us a visit here to try and change my mind. He has our kids but only for the time being and I will never go back to him – never. Just tell him to go home and leave us in peace, unless my brother wants to press charges. I wouldn't blame him if he did," I added.

The officer rubbed his chin. "I guess this is a domestic dispute," he offered. "Mr. Carney, do you wish to press charges?"

"No, officer. Just get this drunk out of my house. I hope he's fit to drive 'cause he's got a ways to go to get back to Westchester."

"Okay, if you're sure." He turned to Al. "Get up and let's get you outa here now. I suggest you stop at the corner and get yourself some strong coffee before you head down the highway."

"There's nothing wrong with me," growled Al, brushing himself off. He turned to me. "You'll be sorry for this, Joan. You'll be real sorry you left me. You'll pay for this – you'll see."

I turned away from him and went to help my brother. "Thank you, officer. I'm sorry we had to trouble you."

The policeman steered Al through the door and turned. "Good luck, Mrs." I shut the door behind me and waited to hear Al's car leave the driveway before I drew a full breath. It was obvious that he was not going to make things easy for me – not in any sense of the word.

Chapter 26

I awoke before the alarm and began dressing for my first interview at Hitachi Metals America at 10 o'clock. I ate breakfast with Bunny and Chuck and lingered over a second cup of coffee. At 9:00 I decided to leave in case I had any trouble finding the building which was off of I95 going south toward New York City. After a few wrong exits and some elaborate U-turns, I managed to find the building. It was now 9:45 a.m. I parked the car and headed inside to the lobby. HMA was on the third floor I was told so I proceeded to the elevator.

As I exited the elevator I was greeted by a tall young man who announced that he was Tom, the personnel manager, and was expecting me. I was relieved to see that he was American. I followed him to a small office in the back corner of the room and sat down.

"I'm pleased to meet you," he assured me. "I must admit I was not too impressed by your typing test -- they faxed it over from the agency; but your credentials from Katharine Gibbs certainly look promising."

I explained about the typing and elicited a smile from the young man across the desk. "I'd be happy to take another test," I said, "but it probably won't be much better. I promise you that if you give me a week,

I can type anything you give me error free and in a reasonable amount of time. If I don't, you can fire me on the spot and I will understand."

He grinned again. "I think that's fair enough," he said. "Somehow, I don't think you'll disappoint me. I do have to introduce you to Mr. Wakayama, a senior sales rep. He will be your immediate boss and we have to have his approval too."

Tom rose from the chair and crossed the room. "Just wait here a moment," he said. "I'll tell him you're here."

He returned momentarily followed by a slightly built young man with a shock of black hair falling over one eye and a wide grin.

"Ohio go zai mas, Joansan," said the young man bowing low in front of me.

I looked at Tom and he nodded. "Good morning, Mr. Wakayama," I countered.

"You call me Mickey," he said. "That my American name. I sell steel and you be good help to me, okay?"

"Okay," I answered. "I'll do my best."

He looked at me again, nodded at Tom, bowed low and walked back across the room.

"I guess you passed muster," Tom said with a grin. "Will you take the job?"

"Absolutely. When do I start? By the way, what did he say?"

"That was Japanese for good morning, Miss Joan. How about tomorrow at 9:00 a.m.?"

"Tom, you've got yourself a secretary. I'll be here bright and early ready to go. Thank you so much."

As soon as I got home, I called the agency. "I got the job, Louise. I got the job."

"Which one?" she asked. You had two appointments."

"Oh, I didn't even go to Pepsi. I took the job at Hitachi. Being they're Japanese, there won't be much shorthand, if any and I convinced the personnel manager to give me a week to prove myself in the typing department. I start tomorrow."

"Okay," said Louise, "if you're sure that's what you want to do, it's okay with me. Good luck, Joan, and let me know if it doesn't work out. Better start brushing up on your Japanese, my dear."

I called Pat that night to give him the good news. "Boy, that's great news, Joan. You sure didn't waste any time getting a job. I'm really proud of you. Bunny invited me for dinner this weekend so we'll really have something to celebrate. Can't wait to see you, hon. Start practicing your Japanese."

"That's what Louise said," I told him. "See you Saturday, *Foleysan*."

Chapter 27

September 23, 1972 was my first day at Hitachi. Metals America. When I arrived, Tom, the Personnel Manager, was already at his desk shuffling a pile of papers.

"Good morning, Joan," he greeted me. "Please sit down. There has been a slight change in plans since yesterday."

I slumped in the chair he offered me. Mr. *Wakayama must have seen my typing test and changed his mind about Joansan.*

"Mr. Wakayama's temp decided to stay and become a Hitachi employee so he doesn't need a secretary. However, our Traffic Manager, Mr. Yoshida, needs one desperately. So, you will work for him – if that's all right."

"But I don't know anything about traffic, Tom, except how many cars there are on the road when I come to and from work."

"Oh, no. . . . . .no, Joan. You don't understand. We traffic goods, not cars. We ship steel and castings from American ports all over the world to our customers. Mr. Yoshida is the manager of that department and you will be working for him. Let me introduce you."

Tom led the way to a group of desks in the far corner of the room. He stopped in front of the largest one where a sturdy looking Japanese man was talking on the phone in rapid Japanese. The man looked up, muttered something unintelligible into the phone and stood up.

"*Ohio go zai mas*," he said in a soft voice. "Me Yoshidasan. I do traffic. You type; give to me. Okay?"

"Okay," I muttered back. *What have I done? My new boss speaks no English.*

I looked past Yoshidasan and saw that there were two other men and one young girl sitting at desks in this area. The one man rose from his chair.

"I'm Peter, Peter Ortiz," he said. "I'll be training you with the help of Bob and Natalie here. You will be Yoshidasan's secretary but you'll be learning from us."

I put out my hand and he took it immediately. He pointed to the other two people. "This is Bob. He does all the claims. And this is Natalie, she's a traffic clerk and we all work together."

"I'll leave you in Peter's capable hands," Tom said and walked back to his desk.

Natalie and Bob welcomed me to the department and Natalie showed me which desk would be mine. The first thing I saw was the big gleaming Remington electric typewriter in the center of the desk. *I'm gonna make you my friend too whether you like it or not.*

Before I even got the cover off the typewriter, Yoshidasan was at my desk with a sheaf of papers in his hand. "You type; give to me. Okay?"

"Okay," I said, taking the papers from his outstretched hand.

I looked questioningly at Natalie. As soon as Yoshidasan returned to his desk, she came over to help me. He had written his notes on pages from a legal pad. "What are these?" I asked.

"Letters to brokers," Natalie answered. "We have form letters for those. Peter made them up and Yoshida doesn't even know it. Peter runs this department. He just doesn't have the title. They have to have a Japanese in charge of every department, but none of them know anything about traffic. They are all good at sales and accounting but not traffic, so we do the best we can. Peter does know the business and he's great at teaching

too. You'll be fine. Don't worry. In a week you'll be like an old-timer."
I smiled derisively, sat down and pulled the cover off the typewriter. A minute later Natalie returned with a packet of form letters.

"Just copy the appropriate letter and address it to the name he has given you. A sample invoice is there too. You can type that up to go with the letter and fill in the proper amounts according to his notes. Think you can manage these?" she asked with a grin.

"I think so, and thanks, Natalie. I'll give a holler if I have any questions."

I turned now to face the Remington. I gingerly turned it on and was greeted by a rather loud hum. I looked around expecting to see everyone staring at me……waiting for me to make a mistake. Everyone was busily engaged at their desks – either on the phone or sorting through papers. I took out the first sample letter, put a sheet of paper into the machine, and began to type. The keys responded to my touch like magic. I soon realized I didn't have to hit them very hard. I could just touch them lightly and the key would imprint.

Before I knew it, I had typed four letters and their accompanying invoices. I made a few mistakes in the beginning but could correct them easily with the miracle of correcting tape which was loaded on the machine just behind the ribbon. A whole new world was opening up and I was actually enjoying it. I finished all the letters before noon and put them in a neat pile on Yoshidasan's desk for him to sign. I looked around and most of the desks were empty. *Everyone's gone to lunch I guess.* I opened my brown paper bag and took out the sandwich I had brought. I knew there was a coffee machine in a back room so I headed for that to get myself some coffee to go with my lunch. *I'll eat at my desk and practice a bit more on the typewriter.*

I was just biting into the second half of my bologna sandwich when Peter came by.

"I hope you'll get the hang of it and stay awhile," he said grinning shyly. We could sure use someone who catches on quick. If you have any questions, please don't hesitate to ask me."

"I really want to learn this business," I said. "Unlike the young girls working here, I'd like to make it a career. I need this job and I plan to be here for the long term. Anything you can teach me, I'll appreciate. And if I screw up, I hope you'll tell me so I can fix it."

He grinned again. "I like your attitude, Joan. If you really do want to learn, I'll see to it that you get the opportunity."

Natalie and Bob returned from lunch and Natalie stopped at my desk. "I had plans today but if you'd like to, we can go to lunch together tomorrow. There's a cafeteria just next door where most of us go just to get a change of scene, and you're welcome to join us. We take turns driving over and we all meet up in the lobby at noon."

"Sounds good," I answered, "but I don't want to crimp your style. After all, I'm almost old enough to be your mother."

"Don't be silly. We're all in this together. Us Americans are in the minority in case you didn't notice, so we all pretty much stick together. Most of the salesmen are real nice even though it's hard to understand them sometimes. The president is a sweetheart too. You'll meet him by the end of the week when he gets back from Japan."

Natalie was right. Most of the Japanese men were very nice and the girls in the office treated me just like one of them. I felt in my heart that I had made the right choice and would be able to turn this job into a career. If I had more work than I could finish during the regular hours, I stayed later until I got everything done. This did not go unnoticed by the Japanese, as most of them made a habit of staying late. Most of them had no families here so work was all they had to fill their time. They were not used to seeing American women working overtime. Most of the younger girls rushed out of the office as soon as the clock struck five. They soon realized that I had a slightly different work ethic and this stood me in good stead with many of the Japanese managers. I felt secure and appreciated and it was a great feeling.

Chapter 28

The first week of my employment flew by and before it ended I was an accomplished typist. Yoshidasan gave me all my work directly but very few words actually passed between us.

As the months went by and the holidays were approaching, a strange phenomenon began occurring on a regular basis. Almost every morning when I arrived at my desk, I would find an assortment of packages sitting there – all provocatively gift wrapped but with no tags. I asked Yoshidasan about these packages and his answer was, "You take home; I no need."

I wanted to refuse but didn't know what to say to him. After a few days of this gift ritual, I went to Peter. "What am I supposed to do with this stuff?" I asked. "I keep stashing it in our coat closet and I'm running out of room."

Peter grinned. "What did Yoshida say to do?"

I lowered my head, embarrassed, and attempted to mimic my boss. "You take home; I no need." Peter smiled at my poor attempt at mimicry.

"I opened two of them yesterday, Peter, and one was a bottle of scotch and the other a large silver bowl. Where are they coming from and what am I supposed to do with them? I can't take them home. Please tell me what to do."

"The gifts are from trucking companies," said Peter. "They are trying to butter him up so he will give them more business. Our department routes all the freight that comes into the U.S. and that means we pick the mode of transportation—whether it's by train or truck. It's a common practice. Yoshida lives in a walk-up in Manhattan with his current girl friend and can't be bothered with silver bowls and stuff like that."

"But what about the scotch?" I asked.

"Oh, he keeps at least every other one of those, Joan. His desk drawers are full of them; believe me. You only get the overflow."

"Well, I am designating you for the overflow from now on, Peter, so start emptying your drawers right now. And as for the bowls and stuff like that, Natalie and Bob and I will take turns, unless there is something you especially want. Your wife might like a silver bowl, you know."

"No thanks, Joan. You guys split the loot between you. I'll settle for a bottle of booze now and then."

I felt much better after getting that straightened out. We spent lunch time splitting up the loot I had already stashed. Bob and Natalie were thrilled to be the recipients of some free gifts, and we got our closet space back.

The holidays came and went and time continued to fly by. In March Peter informed me that Traffic School was starting at the World Trade Center in New York City, and if I wanted to enroll in the evening classes, he would get it approved. Mr. Hiromoto, who was the Head of the Personnel Dept., called me into his office one afternoon.

"Peter tells me you want go to school and learn traffic. Is this true?"

"Yes Hiromotosan, it is true. I want to learn everything I can about trafficking freight."

"You not mind drive to Manhattan?"

"No, I don't mind driving to the City. I will go only one night a week to school so that's not too bad." I paused, waiting for him to speak.

"I will approve," he said with a smile. "I hope you be with us long time, Joansan, so money not wasted on you."

"I hope so too, Hiromotosan, and thank you very much."

I smiled and rose from my chair. Hiromotosan bowed and then, with a little hesitation, extended his hand. "I must learn be more American."

We shook hands and I returned to my desk. At the first opportunity I went to find Peter.

"Thank you for giving me the chance to go to school and for convincing Hiromoto to pay for it. I will work hard. I promise. I'll have to leave the office by 4 o'clock on the day I have school because classes start at 6 o'clock and I'll need extra time to find a parking place under Riverside Drive."

"That's not a problem. Hiromoto is sending Yoshida a memo to that effect so stop worrying. Classes don't start for two weeks so you have time to work out your schedule for the day you leave early. I've already registered you for the semester, so you're all set."

I was so excited when I got home that night and told Chuck and Bunny about going to school. My next call was to Pat to share my good fortune with him as well. He was thrilled for me. Chuck gave me detailed directions on how to get there and even offered to drive down there on the weekend so I could see first hand where I had to go.

Finding a parking space in downtown Manhattan did not pose a problem but getting from the car to the Trade Center on foot was daunting. Riverside Drive itself was closed to traffic for repairs that year so the streets under it were pretty well deserted. My first night was a doozy. I saw two winos sleeping in doorways on West Street and a panhandling bum approached me on Wall Street. He followed me for half a block, begging for money, and I was terrified.

I had been told that this end of town, which was known as the battery, was not too safe for a woman alone at night, but I didn't realize how scary it would be until I began attending classes. After I reported back to Peter and Natalie about my hair-raising experience, they sent me off the next week with a can of mace in my pocket, a whistle around my neck and a resolve to be alert to everything around me. I had a few more Alfred Hitchcock moments that year but got through the semester without mishap and thanked God for this as no one else deserved the credit.

Attending Traffic School provided some other challenges as well, and one of these was taking the express elevator to the 46th floor of the Trade Center. This ride came as a close second to the roller coaster ride at our local amusement park, Playland in Rye. The first time I took this trip it was several minutes before my stomach joined me at the next bank of elevators to continue my journey. My classroom was on the 67th floor so the next leg of my upward journey was often agonizingly slow as people were exiting on almost every floor on the way up. When the sign illuminated at 67, I drew a sigh of relief and stepped out into the hall. It took a minute or two to get my breath and gather my sense of direction. I found my classroom and took a seat by the window.

Before I had a chance to take in my surroundings, the instructor entered the room and introduced himself. It was then that I noticed that, although the room was quite full, there was only one other person seated in the row I was in. Most of the students were taking seats near the wall and closer to the door. The reason for these seating choices soon became apparent when I saw a helicopter outside my window and met the pilot's eyes with my own; I thought I would pass out. Obviously, many of the students had attended classes here before and were aware of the horrors of being up so high. In the week that followed several people had to give up the class because they could not take the height. After about a month in this tower of learning, seeing planes next to my window became commonplace and I barely looked up anymore.

Occasionally, if he had to work late, Pat would meet me after class and we would ride home together. I enjoyed having someone to share the ride home with and loved to regale him with some of the weird goings-on outside my classroom window. About once a month Peter would let me leave early to go to class and I would meet Pat for lunch in Manhattan. Sometimes we would walk through SoHo like tourists and other times we would spend an hour or two at the Metropolitan Museum of Art – one of our favorite places. I began to look forward to these special times, and our relationship prospered under this umbrella of shared activities.

Pat was more than just my best friend; he was an important part of my life. He had become friends with Peter by now and was also included as a guest at many of our HMA functions. The Japanese executives liked him very much and enjoyed his wonderful sense of humor. I was proud to be on the arm of this attractive and successful business man.

Al and I almost never went out to dinner (except with my parents or on our anniversary) and he had never enjoyed parties or gatherings with people he did not know, so this was quite a change of pace for me. Pat often took me out to lunch or dinner and introduced me as "his lady" at formal events hosted by American Express at the Waldorf Astoria on Park Avenue. I was seeing a side of life I had never been exposed to before, and I must confess, I loved every minute of it.

Chapter 29

During this first year at the Traffic Academy we had an interesting occurrence at HMA, which changed the course of my career and ultimately my life.

My quiet, unassuming boss, Yoshidasan, stole a rather large claim check destined for the Canadian Government, gathered his Puerto Rican girlfriend and her two kids from their Manhattan apartment and took off in his company car for the West Coast. He also had his company American Express card in his wallet which he did not hesitate to use at the slightest whim. His rash spending habits were his eventual undoing as the company and American Express could trace his purchases and find his location. The police picked him up in San Francisco and he ended up being deported back to Japan where he was sentenced to a rather lengthy prison term for embezzlement. Mr. Hiromoto was heartbroken as he had sponsored this young man in the U.S. and thought of him as a son.

This left the Traffic Dept. without a manager, and so it was incumbent on Mr. Hiromoto to do the only sensible thing -- make Peter Ortiz the manager of the Traffic Dept. I was thrilled at this turn of events because Peter was (and had been) the true manager of the department for as long as I had been there and this made him the first American manager in the corporate office. His first official act as manager was to promote me to Asst. Traffic Manager which made me the first woman to ever have the word manager after her name, even if it was assistant. What a cause for celebration!

And so we did. Peter took us all out to dinner that night and was pleased and proud to pay for the meal with his brand new company American Express Card.

The next year seemed to fly by. Business was very good and our department was busier than ever. With Pat's help I found an apartment in Eastchester and was now living on my own in an area equidistant from my kids and my office. Elyse and I had made peace after the first year of our separation. When Al moved his girl friend into the house in Bronxville, my eldest daughter knew for sure that mommy was not the real culprit in her parents' separation. Daddy fell off his holy pedestal and my daughter and I became friends again.

It had been a terrible shock to me and to my children to discover that the man Aunt Jean had been having an affair with was my husband and their beloved, daddy. Despite his many past infidelities Jean had fallen hopelessly in love with Al and apparently, the feeling was mutual. Pat was temporarily rendered speechless also when he was confronted with this unlikely truth, but soon we all accepted the inevitable. After giving the situation a little thought, Pat remembered wondering where Jean had been going to put so many miles on the car. Now he realized she had been driving to Mineola, L. I. to have lunch with her lover several times a week. Even her charge account bills had been climbing he recalled; and for someone who spent little on clothes or makeup, this too was a mystery. Now, of course, it all began to make sense. A woman in love – Jean was following a whole new pattern.

It was a bit of a shock to Al's mother when he moved Jean into the house as my replacement. She had assumed that I was the one carrying on an affair. Now she had to accept that her son was living in sin with his wife's former best friend. I almost felt sorry for her.

Meanwhile, Pat and I continued our relationship as best friends. Then, on one of those afternoons when Peter let me leave for class early, I parked at the Trade Center and took the short subway ride uptown to meet Pat at an Argentinean restaurant on the outskirts of SoHo. We had wanted to try this eatery for some time now and my mouth was watering for the delicious steak he had assured me we would enjoy there.

After a sensational meal he took me to the apartment of one of his business friends. I was a bit apprehensive but went along with it – mostly out of curiosity. He said we were celebrating his divorce from Jean which was now final. He had been teasing me lately about being "his lady" and said we needed some private time. I was very fond of Pat but honestly never thought of him as anything but my best friend until very recently. When we arrived at the flat, Pat opened a bottle of wine and invited me into the bedroom. Before I knew what was happening, we were in each other's arms and I was experiencing feelings I never knew I was capable of. After all, I was frigid – always had been.

It soon became apparent that in Pat's arms, I was cured of my frigidity and was actually experiencing ecstasy for the first time in my life. Love and physical gratification had found their way into my life at long last, and I embraced them completely. Needless to say, our relationship took on a whole new dimension after that fateful afternoon, and I learned the meaning of true love for the first time in my life.

A few months later Pat asked me to marry him. I loved him unreservedly, but marriage was not something I wanted to consider so I said no and begged him to understand. In the eyes of the church I was still married and I could not afford to fight Al in court for the divorce he had been reluctant to give me. I considered getting an annulment and Fr. Bill at Graymoor encouraged me in this effort, especially because he was serving on the Diocesan Tribunal. I needed two witnesses who knew me before and after my marriage to testify on my behalf that our union was not sacramental. Both dear friends (Carol and Maria) who would have stood by me died that year and I was left with no witnesses to attest to the difficulties I encountered when marrying an agnostic husband who did not want his children to be brought up Catholic. This attitude almost canceled the ceremony permanently, but at the last minute, he had reneged and signed the papers the church required in the case of mixed marriage.

And so, I turned Pat down because being a Roman Catholic was (and still is) too important for me to give up. Pat was Catholic too so knew that the Church did not recognize marriage after divorce, but his faith was not as strict as mine. I tried to convince him of my love and how honored he should be that I was with him completely without benefit of a piece of paper. That worked for a few years, but eventually it would be our downfall. For the time being, however, we were as happy as newlyweds.

We agreed to maintain our separate apartments because of the children, but I spent most of my weekends at his place. We did some extensive traveling to Europe, courtesy of his boss and American Express Travel & Leisure magazine, and generally had a wonderful and fulfilling life together. Our collective children all got along and continued to maintain their friendships so that made our relationship even more like that of a family. I was happier than I had ever been in my life and my love for Pat grew with intensity and fervor.

Chapter 30

During my time with Pat I had a life changing experience. He was Catholic also and had recently gone back to church and we often attended mass together. I was feeling rather uncomfortable going to communion because I knew I was committing adultery – a very big sin in the Catholic Church, and Pat was aware of my discomfort although he did not agree with it.

There was a strong religious movement in Westchester County at the time known as *Cursillo* and Pat became involved. He went on an all male weekend at one of the churches further up in the county.

Cursillo in Christianity is a movement that, through a method of its own and with God's grace, manages to enable the essential realities of the Christian to come to life in the uniqueness, originality, and creativity of each person. In becoming aware of their potential and while accepting their limitations they exercise their freedom by their conviction. They strengthen their will with their decision to propitiate friendship in virtue of their constancy in both their personal and community life. The *Cursillo* Movement consists of proclaiming the best news of the best reality: that God, in Christ, loves us.

Pat enjoyed the weekend so much and was so sure that it was just what I needed, that he made arrangements for me to attend the next *Cursillo* for women and offered to be my sponsor. I was excited about the prospect of a religious retreat and agreed immediately. He would tell me nothing about what would go on so I was unable to form any realistic expectations. He drove me there one Friday night a few weeks later and said he would pick me up again late Sunday afternoon when it concluded. With a kiss and a hug he left me at the door and drove away.

Even now I find it difficult to describe the initial experience. There were thirty five women attending. All but one were married. One lady was divorced and then there was me. I admitted to being separated but everyone accepted me for who I was and not the condition of my marital state. We had group meetings and group meals and time to meditate. There was noise and extreme quiet and lots of love. By Saturday afternoon many tears had been shed, laughs shared and problems openly discussed. We had bonded like long-lost sisters. At four o'clock we were all to go to confession in preparation for receiving communion at Sunday Mass. I was terrified! *How was I going to confess being an adulteress? What could I say to the Priest so that he would give me absolution? How could I face him with such a big sin on my soul? Maybe I won't even go……………*

Three forty-five came and all the women were leaving the dorm to go to church for confession. I sat on the end of my bed trying to decide what to do. My divorced friend, Dora, came over and sat down next to me.

"I know what's wrong, Joan, just by looking at your face. Please come with us. It will be alright; I promise."

Dora knew my story well as did most of the women there as all our secrets had come out in our group sessions. She put her arms around me and pulled me to my feet." I'll be with you every step of the way. Remember, I'm divorced and I'm not afraid to tell him."

I smiled wanly and followed her down the hall and across the yard into the church. There was already a long line formed at each of the two confessionals. We joined one of the lines and waited our turn.

When my turn came my hands were ice cold but I was determined not to be afraid. I entered the confessional, knelt down and murmured the obligatory prayer. "Bless me Father for I have sinned . . . . " After muttering a few minor offences like missing mass or eating meat on Friday, I proceeded to tell the Monsignor (he had told me who he was) that I was separated and sleeping with a divorced man. You could have cut the silence with a knife. After a huge pause, he spoke.

"That makes you an adulteress, my child. Do you understand that?

"Yes, Monsignor, I do, but I would like to explain the circumstances."

"Go on," he answered briskly.

I explained the situation including the fact that the man in question had sponsored me at this *Cursillo*. I reiterated that he was divorced and had asked me to marry him. I also mentioned that I was unable thus far to get a divorce as my husband had refused to sign the papers.

The Monsignor's voice was low and reedy but he minced no words. "Have you thought of getting an annulment?" he demanded. All you have to do is go to the Brooklyn Diocese and apply. The cost is about $5,000, I believe. That is the only way you can turn your life around and be free of sin."

"I cannot afford an annulment, Monsignor," I responded. The tears were starting to form now. "I can barely support myself and my children."

"Then I cannot help you, my child, and I cannot give you absolution. You are no longer welcome in the Catholic Church and you will never again be able to receive communion. Please leave the confessional."

I was aghast. I could not believe that a priest had said this to me. I had expected a lecture but I did not expect to be excommunicated. I stood up and walked out into the church. I saw Dora immediately but turned away and almost ran down the aisle. I had to be alone just now.

Mass was scheduled for 11:00 a.m. Sunday morning. I told Dora what had happened when we met for breakfast at 8:00 a.m. She was appalled but insisted I should not take it to heart. "The Monsignor is an old man, Joan, and way behind the times. After mass we can go find Fr. Tim. He's a young priest and I'm sure he will be able to help you. Don't worry any more about it now. Let's just get ready for Mass."

We filed into the church at 10:45 and took our places on 35 chairs that were arranged in a semi circle in front of the altar. I kept thinking someone was going to come up to me and ask me to leave, but no one did. As the bell rang announcing the beginning of mass, the big church doors opened and a procession of men entered holding lit candles and white lilies. They processed down the aisle and took their seats in the pews opposite us. I realized immediately they were the women's husbands and my dear Pat was among them. Dora's boyfriend was there too and suddenly all the women were crying. No one had known that they would be at the mass and emotions were running high. Some of the men grinned and Pat raised his hand in a gentle wave. My heart sank. What would he think when I was the only woman unable to go to the rail to receive communion?

The Mass began and before I knew it, it was time for communion. The women rose, row by row, and walked to the rail. When my row rose, I stayed seated with my head bowed. The women came back one by one and Dora stopped in front of me. I looked up. She looked down at me and with a straight face and tears in her eyes she said, "the body of Christ" and put her communion wafer into my open mouth. In a reflex action, I took it on my tongue, said "Amen" and lowered my head. .No one said a word but I knew many people had seen this, including Pat. I could not believe anyone, especially someone I barely knew, could do such a remarkable thing for me. I was overwhelmed with feelings.

As soon as Mass ended and people stood up to leave I grabbed Dora and hugged her so hard. We both began crying and I was at a loss for words. "God bless you," was all I could think of to say and before I could say any more, Pat was at my side too, flanked by Dora's boyfriend. They both hugged Dora too and we all went down the aisle together and out into the courtyard at the side of the church. Dora suggested again that I find Fr. Tim and Pat said he would take me to him himself. He and the young priest had really bonded during Pat's Cursillo and he knew he would straighten this out. I thanked Dora again and vowed to see her before I left and Pat and I left to find Fr. Tim.

We caught up with the priest in the great hall helping to set up the refreshments for the closing reception. Pat introduced me and asked Fr. Tim if he could give us a few minutes of his time. The priest agreed and we went into a small office down the hall from the festivities. When we got to the room Pat informed me that he would wait for me outside as I might want to have confession again. I looked at him questioningly and then at the priest. "Good idea," said Fr. Tim. "We'll see you shortly. Save us some punch and cookies, Pat, ok?" Pat grinned and closed the door.

"Well now," said Fr. Tim, just tell me what happened in the confessional yesterday, but first let me pour you a cup of coffee and light you a cigarette. Just relax and let it all out. I just want to listen right now."

As I sipped the coffee and took a long drag on the cigarette, I felt myself relax. I began slowly and then told Fr. Tim what had transpired in the confessional with the Monsignor. He did not interrupt but just listened until I was all done. Then he patted my hand and spoke.

"The Monsignor is 89 years old, Joan and has been retired for some time. He was filling in today just for confessions and that, apparently, was a mistake on our part. He is of the old school and a bit behind the times. I am so sorry you were treated this way. I, on the other hand, am of the new school of priests. Some may say too liberal but I don't think so. It's obvious that God means as much to you as he always did, if not more, and not going to church and receiving the sacraments is inconceivable to you. I understand your problem and the church should too. You and all divorced Catholics are still welcome in the church and never forget that. Now, put out your cigarette, finish your coffee, and give me a good confession."

In five minutes I received absolution and was the happiest women in the world. I thanked Father from the bottom of my heart and together we went out to find Pat and celebrate the end of a beautiful weekend.

Chapter 31

Though Al had refused to give me a divorce these past years, he was finally forced into submission six years later when he and Jean bought some property in Massachusetts and the State insisted that his wife's name must be on the deed. That did not bode well with Jean who was putting up half the money so it forced Al to finally divorce me. He paid for the divorce but I got absolutely nothing from it – not even the back money he owed me from the original separation. His lawyer had the judge expunge all past debts to me and, since I did not attend the proceeding to protest, I was granted nothing. By now I was able to care for myself without his help, so I mentally cleaned the slate and prepared to start my life over in earnest.

When Elyse graduated from high school and turned nineteen in the fall, I helped her get into Berkley Business School in Purchase, just down the street from HMA. She moved in with me in my studio apartment in Eastchester and we became roommates. I was still seeing Pat then and by now our relationship had escalated into one of deep and abiding affection. I spent some nights at Pat's who had an apartment several blocks from mine but other than that we still maintained separate households.

Ali, now fifteen, joined our household when Al threw her out of the house for 'behavior unbecoming his daughter.' This is how he usually handled our kids when they displeased him. She moved in with Elyse and me and, though crowded in the small studio apartment, the girls didn't seem to mind sharing a pull-out couch in the living room. I slept on a daybed in an alcove on the way to the kitchen. It was tight but somehow it worked. We bonded.

Brett, unable to live in peace with his father and the woman he knew as Aunt Jean, moved in with one of his high school friends, much to his grandmother's dismay. This left only Beth in the Bronxville house. I think part of her loved having her father to herself for once, but another part hated being left behind by her mother and sisters. She knew that as soon as Elyse got her own apartment, she would replace her and come live with Ali and me. This is precisely what happened a year later when Elyse graduated from Berkley and got a job in nearby New Rochelle. She found an apartment in the same complex we were in and now my roommate became my neighbor. *God does indeed work in mysterious ways.*

Under great objection from Al, I moved Beth into my apartment and we were all one big happy family again. I started to think about getting a bigger place for us but knew it would take some looking to find one that I could afford that would be big enough for the three of us.

I managed to see Brett fairly often and Pat and I even took him and the girls bowling on several occasions. My kids all loved Pat so that made things much easier all around. He and Ali had developed a very special relationship. Even when she was very sad and would not talk to any of us, she would talk to him. In many ways he was more of a father to her than her own had been.

All our lives seemed to be going well until the summer of 1978 when suddenly things between Pat and I began to disintegrate. He seemed to be going through 'a change of life' – rather early for a man in his early 50's. He'd had a mild heart attack the previous year and that seemed to set off a chain of events that ended with me calling it quits and breaking up with him. I loved him with all my heart but he was becoming so jealous and untrusting that I could not bear it. He accused me of all sorts of infidelities…. even with men in his own company. I still did not want to marry again and thought he had accepted this, but soon found I was mistaken. He wanted that piece of paper more than ever -- like an ownership lease to which I could not comply. The end came abruptly and sadly. I regretted my actions as soon as I had broken it off, but he refused to take me back. Three months later he married a girl a year younger than his oldest daughter. That act tore me apart and it took several months to recover from this change in my otherwise happy existence. My kids were my salvation and their love is what kept me going after losing the only man I had ever really loved. I thought I would die from the loss, but it's amazing how life goes on and wounds eventually heal.

Soon after that huge change in my life, Elyse announced she was getting married. She had been dating Kevin since she was sixteen and now they wanted to tie the knot. She asked Ali to be her maid of honor, and on the day of the wedding Ali announced that she would be getting married too --a mere three weeks hence. I was flabbergasted! Pat accompanied me to Elyse's wedding but it was merely a courtesy for old time's sake. By the time Ali's day came I was alone once again. Al refused to walk her down the aisle or contribute to the wedding in any way so my brother offered to give the bride away. Secretly, he was thrilled at the prospect and was delighted that the father of the bride was not to participate. Unfortunately, plans went awry. Al came to the wedding at the last minute and insisted on walking his daughter down the aisle. My poor brother was devastated, but what could I do?

We did not expect to see Al at the reception but in he came just as the strains of "Daddy's Little Girl" emanated from the bandstand. I thought my heart would break for Ali as her eyes searched the room for her father, but when he entered the hall and walked up to the bride's table, her face lit up and I knew it would be alright. I hated him for putting her through this but it was worth it to see her smile up at her daddy.

By this time Beth was also romantically involved. When she graduated high school she too went to a small business school in White Plains and within months had moved into an apartment with the young man in question who worked at General Foods in White Plains where Ali was already employed and where Beth also hoped to get a job.

I was entirely alone for the first time in my tiny studio apartment which now seemed huge with only me living there. Another new phase of my life was beginning.

Chapter 32

～⚭～

God took a hand in my life once again. Business at HMA was booming and I was so busy I had no time to spend feeling sorry for myself. I had completed all the courses at the Traffic Academy as well as others the company encouraged me to take and was feeling very confident in my chosen career.

And then another miracle occurred. Peter promoted me to Traffic Manager. I was floored but gratified beyond belief. No woman had ever been promoted to management in Hitachi up to now. I would be the first woman manager ever. I was thrilled! I never worked so hard in my life and loved every minute of it. With the kids out on their own and Pat out of my life, I had no reason to hurry home, so I worked a lot of overtime which was appreciated not only by Peter but by Mr. Hiromoto as well.

He called Peter and I into his office one day and informed us that, since it is customary for all managers to make a trip to Japan to tour our facilities and mingle with other international managers, I am expected to make the next trip which will be two months hence. Peter had made the trip the year before and was excited for me to have this opportunity so soon after being promoted. I could hardly contain myself and thanked

Mr. Hiromoto profusely. It took me the rest of the day to really take this in, and when I realized that I would be the first woman to make this trip, I had all I could do to control my enthusiasm. I couldn't wait to tell the girls, and when I did, they were just as excited for me as I was.

On top of this huge announcement, the work load increased beyond belief. We were so busy I didn't see how I could be out of the office for three weeks traveling in Japan. Peter felt the pressure too and met with Mr. Hiromoto to discuss getting some help in our department.

It was finally agreed that we would hire another clerk, and this time we asked for a Japanese girl so she could translate the telexes we received daily from Japan. Mr. Hiromoto was not pleased with this request as Japanese women were not considered suitable for office work. Japanese women in the work place were still frowned upon by Japanese men. 'A woman's place is in the home' -- arranging flowers and learning to play a musical instrument was the accepted course of action.

Peter had a long talk with Hiromoto and even spoke with the President and convinced them that this was a legitimate request. We hired a young Japanese exchange student who had just graduated from college in Connecticut and now lived in White Plains. Her name was Misako and she was the most beautiful Asian girl I had ever seen. She was to report to me and we became fast friends almost immediately.

Misako was not only bright but gutsy too. Some of the young Japanese trainees in the sales department were actually intimidated by her. She spoke perfect English but could converse brilliantly in her native tongue so the men could no longer talk freely in front of her as they were used to doing -- a trait that used to infuriate me. They would speak in Japanese right in front of us and not consider it rude at all. Misako soon changed that. They were forced to speak English when dealing with our department, but occasionally Misako would let fly with her own brand of Japanese slang which infuriated some of the younger men. I had to caution her to be discreet or she might find herself out of a job. She knew I was right and tried very hard to keep her temper and not show any disrespect to any of the Japanese executives. She caught on quickly to all the ins and outs of moving freight from the various ports of call to our customers. She respected Peter's abilities and got along with him very well. She absorbed knowledge like a sponge and I soon began to relax about my upcoming trip to Japan. I turned my attention to what I would be packing and also worked on some basic Japanese language skills that I hoped would stand me in good stead.

Before I knew it, the day arrived. Peter took me to JFK where I flew all alone non-stop to Tokyo. The flight was an unbelievable sixteen hours, and I was never so glad to set down on land in my entire life. I was met in Tokyo by one of the Japanese men who had spent a year in our accounting department in the New York Corporate Office. He helped me get through Customs and even carried my bag for me. He then put me in a taxi, stuffed some Yen into the driver's hand and told him in rapid Japanese where to take me. He told me I would be staying in Hitachi Metals' private hotel which would be my home base during my visit to Japan.

Forty minutes later, having driven through heavy rush-hour traffic, the taxi stopped in front of a large concrete building in what appeared to be an area similar to Times Square in Manhattan. There were neon lights everywhere and crowds of people walking in every direction. I searched the street signs for a clue to my whereabouts, but they were all in Japanese with no English subtitles whatever. I gestured to the driver and in very broken Japanese asked where I was. *Ginza* was his response. *Ah so* was my answer. And so my adventure began in earnest.

"You John??" The man who opened the door scratched his head and looked at me strangely.

"No," I said, shaking my head vehemently. And then it hit me. I suddenly realized that all the telexes I had received from Japan these past months were addressed to John Greene. After the first few attempts at correction went unnoticed I refrained from further ones. After all, I knew there was no equivalent for Joan in the Japanese language and I didn't really care what they called me as long as they did as I requested. I never dreamed this oversight would come back to haunt me.

"I am Joan, Joan Greene from Hitachi Metals in New York. Mr. Hiromoto sent me."

This elicited a huge grin from the rather short, rotund man who was beckoning me to enter. "You girl" . . . . . . snicker, snicker.

"Off shoes, Joansan. No shoes in house. Put on sandal."

He pointed to a rack of shelves next to the front door. Every shelf was covered with sandals – all of the same style and color but in a variety of sizes. Some were rather large (for a full grown man I thought) and some were small enough for a young boy or someone like me. I pointed to a smallish pair that looked like they would fit me, and the proprietor grabbed them and thrust them at me, grinning all the while.

"Leave shoe here." He pointed at the floor under the shelves. "Or take to room if want. You only girl here – no one will take."

I took in the last sentence with fear and trembling. *I was the only girl here.* Peter had told me there would be eighteen managers here for this meeting – eight from the U. S. and ten from various branch offices in Europe, the Far East and South America. I knew the names of several of the U. S. managers and had even spoken to some of them by phone before we all embarked on this trip. At least they would speak English. In truth, being the only woman had not even occurred to me.

The proprietor, Mr. Wakimoto, pointed to the elevator, picked up my suitcase and escorted me to my room on the seventh floor. When we arrived at my door he opened it and then handed me a large brass key. "Dinner on floor two at seven o'clock. You rest till then, Joansan."

"Domo arigato," I murmured in my best Japanese and closed the door behind me.

The room was sparse, but very clean. There was a single bed with a reasonably hard mattress containing one blanket and a pillow. A small wooden dresser with a mirror stood opposite the bed and a sink and towel rack occupied the other wall of the narrow room. The small closet held a kimono made of cotton which I assumed was to be used as a robe or a dressing gown. All in all it was adequate – certainly not luxurious, but sufficient.

I flopped on the bed and closed my eyes. When I opened them again my watch said six o'clock. I went out into the hall and found a bathroom a few doors down. As I entered I noticed the urinal on the wall and several sets of stalls. I opted for the latter and made use of the facilities. I had a sneaking suspicion that this was either a men's room only or, since I was a woman, it was now considered gender indifferent. So far I was the only occupant but who knew how long that would last. Remembering the sink in my room, I opted for a rapid return to privacy and left as quickly as my sandaled feet would carry me. A sigh of relief escaped me as I closed the door behind me and walked to the sink where I could wash my hands and face in total anonymity.

I decided not to change for dinner but just smoothed out the slacks and jacket of my traveling attire. I hung up the other pairs of pants I had packed along with the few shirts and an additional jacket and put the other items of clothing in the dresser drawers. We had been told to bring an extra overnight-type bag for short hops between manufacturing facilities, and I stowed that in the closet as well. Having completed all my ablutions, I headed out the door to the elevator which I hoped would take me to the dining room on the second floor.

I was not the first person to arrive for dinner and the cacophony of sounds that came from the dining room assured me that I was in the right place. Most of the words that assaulted my eardrums were not English, although I did detect a few recognizable phrases as I meandered across the room in search of an empty seat. I spotted two men who appeared to be conversing in English and headed in their direction. There was an empty seat to the left of one of them and I claimed it as my own. I surveyed the room. Realizing that I was, in truth, the only woman present, I tried to introduce myself to the man on my right. He turned immediately, thrust out his hand and suddenly fell silent.

"Whoa, you're a girl," he stammered in fluent English. "We were told there might be one woman manager here, but frankly, we didn't believe it. You must be John," he grinned. "When we get telex copies in Chicago, it always shows the addressee as John. You and I have talked on the phone, Joan, but I never realized you were a manager. I assumed you were a secretary. They don't usually promote women. You must be pretty special." He paused to look me over. "Oh, by the way, my name is Ken, Ken Allen from the Chicago office."

Ken poked the man next to him and introduced him to me as Jack Kemp from the Detroit office. Jack did a double take and then smiled from ear to ear. We shook hands and I began to feel more comfortable. As the evening progressed we met several of the other attendees. Many of them were from Europe and South America where one of our biggest customers, Gillette, had several facilities. Most of them spoke English as a second language and we were able to converse quite easily. They were as surprised to find a woman in their midst as my U.S. compatriots. As it turned out there were only two or three managers representing Far Eastern offices, and they spoke very little English. It would be part of our jobs, we were told, to overcome this discrepancy and find ways to open communication with them and share ideas. We were all made aware that this would be much more than just a cultural experience, but one that would mandate creativity, patience and hard work. I love a challenge and this was certainly going to be a memorable one.

A distinguished Japanese gentleman entered the dining room and seated himself at the head of the table. He introduced himself as our host for this visit and advised that we would be visiting Hitachi's corporate headquarters tomorrow. There would be a meeting of all attendees followed by a luncheon, and we would be given the entire schedule for our upcoming visit. His next remarks shocked us all. We would not be going to this meeting in taxis or company cars, but via the subway just like any other Japanese employee. We were to experience the culture and customs of the country first hand. We were instructed to meet in the lobby of the hotel at eight o'clock sharp to meet our escort. He would help us familiarize ourselves with the subway procedure because of the language barrier. After that, we were informed, "You are on your own."

At the end of the meal our host dismissed us with the suggestion that we get a good night's rest and prepare to enjoy our first day in Tokyo tomorrow. Breakfast is at seven he added. We filed out, quietly, like dutiful lambs, each to our own room and deep in thought about the coming day's events.

Chapter 33

My first breakfast in Japan will live with me in infamy as long as I live. As I entered the breakfast room, which was located one floor down from the lobby, I immediately realized the reason for its rather out-of-the-way location. The odor that assailed my nostrils was almost impossible to describe. All I could disseminate was the strong aroma of fish.

I stopped inside the door and tried to get my bearings. The room was grey in color and very long with a narrow counter under rows of small vertical windows running down the entire left side. Some of the windows were raised and some were not. I could see plates of food extending out on the counters where the windows were open.

After further investigation, it appeared that the room was divided into two sections. Both sections were comprised of long tables and benches (prison-style I mused) but the section in the rear of the room was full of young Japanese men in business suits. All heads were bent down into bowls of food which I could not yet distinguish. The front section was not full and contained several of the faces I had seen the night before, including my new friends from Chicago and Detroit. I headed in their direction. They looked up as I sat down and welcomed me to yet another cultural experience.

"How do you like the smell?" Ken asked, nodding toward the rear of the room. "You'll never guess what it is they are eating," he added.

"It's fish heads and rice," Jack announced rather too loudly. "That's why it smells so bad in here."

"What are they serving us?" I inquired, feeling a wave of nausea sweep over me.

"Oh, don't worry, Joan. We're getting good ole American bacon and eggs I think. At least that's what it looks like when the windows come up on this end," Jack clarified.

I smiled in relief and wondered how I could ignore the smell enough to get down the bacon and eggs I now saw being placed on the counter nearest our section. The window was raised and the guys went running. I followed slowly from behind and gingerly picked up a plate. A big pot of coffee was already on our table and so I kept busy pouring for the three of us – prolonging the actual act of eating till the last possible minute. Then hunger came to the fore and I picked up my fork. It didn't taste half bad when you could get past the odor that permeated everything in the room. I told myself I would get used to it –after all we would be here for almost three weeks.

When breakfast ended we all went back to our rooms for the last minute ablutions before heading out on our first official day in Tokyo. We all met in the lobby of the hotel twenty minutes later. Mr. Wakimoto greeted me and turned back to his list. I looked around for Ken and Jack and spotted them coming down the stairs. They saw me too and headed in my direction. Mr. Wakimoto clapped his hands to get our attention and the room went silent. He quickly introduced another Japanese man – well dressed and looking every inch a budding executive, who addressed the group in excellent English.

"I am Nayakisan. I will be your guide for the day. Please feel free to ask me any questions. We are now going out as a group, so please try not to get lost. Pick a buddy to walk with, especially when we get to the subway as it will be very crowded." Jack and Ken looked at me and gave the thumbs up. I followed suit and whispered, "the three musketeers." They grinned and nodded in agreement.

"I spent a lot of time on the New York subways so I should be a pro at this," I announced to my two male companions.

"I hear they are a bit more crowded than we're used to," offered Jack. "Just stay close and we'll be fine," said Ken and off we went.

We followed. Nayakisan out the door and around the corner to the subway entrance. I noted the name of the station – in Japanese of course. As we went down the steps I saw a map of the subway system, colorized just like in New York, but the station names were all in Japanese. I looked for the name of the one we had just left, but they all looked pretty much the same. As we got to the platform a train was just pulling in. Nayakisan said, "As soon as the people get off, you get on at once."

Jack mumbled, "it feels like we're preparing for a scrimmage on the football field." Before Ken or I could respond, we were being pushed forcibly onto the subway car. I felt a sharp stab in my back. A man with a huge paddle was pushing the crowd into the train. I could see our reflection in the windows beyond the door. He held the paddle against the backs of the onrushing mob and pushed as hard as he could, grunting all the time, until the doors of the train closed.

The train began to move but I could not move. I was literally wedged into this mass of humanity like a steer in a cattle car. I tried to look around but could barely turn my head. I spied Jack out of the corner of my eye and tried to speak but just as I opened my mouth, a nearby elbow closed it. The elbow belonged to Ken and all I could think was, "thank God."

"Two more stations," he muttered. "Nayaki told me just as we got on."

"Thanks," I stammered as the train lurched to a stop at the next station. I began to edge toward the door closest to me where I saw people disembarking so I would be ready to get off. Ken pushed himself into line behind me and when the train stopped we literally charged out the door. I looked around the platform and saw Jack squeezing through another door and several others from our group following behind him including Mr. Nayaki. He walked over to the wall and looked around for his sheep. He began checking names off his clip board and then signaled for us to follow him up a flight of stairs a short way down the platform. I looked up and noted the name of the station. In brackets under the name were the names of several companies; among them was Hitachi, Ltd, our destination.

We climbed the stairs Nayakisan indicated, but before reaching the top where we could see daylight, we turned right in a tunnel that took us directly into the corporate offices of Hitachi Metals, Ltd. Nayakisan led us to the elevators and we followed him to the fourteenth floor. From there we were herded into a huge conference room set up much like a classroom would be. We took seats, and after looking around, I realized that our group was considerably smaller than yesterday.

Nayakisan welcomed us to the corporate office and explained that this meeting would be for the English-speaking members only. Our Japanese and other far Eastern members would be meeting elsewhere today. This meeting would be an orientation and an opportunity for us to meet some of the executives of the International Division. By the time we left today we would be given our travel itinerary and a summary of the activities we would be sharing throughout our visit to the several manufacturing plants of Hitachi Metals, Ltd.

Nayakisan was true to his word. We learned a lot that day, not only about Hitachi but also about ourselves. At about 10:30 a.m. several lovely young ladies came into the meeting dressed in identical gray uniforms and served us tea at our desks. The interlude took all of fifteen minutes and it was back to business as usual. Being the only woman in the group, I took this opportunity to ask one of the young ladies where I cold find the rest room. She gave me directions in broken English and I made my way out the door and down the hall.

I entered a large square room with two stalls. I opened the door to the first stall and was horrified to find only an empty space with a hole in the middle of the floor. I closed the door and moved on to the next stall. It was exactly the same. I was momentarily at a loss. After all I was in a business suit with a skirt, pantyhose and three inch heels. I realized immediately that I would have to remove not only my shoes but my pantyhose as well. I did so, placing the items on the floor near the wall. I returned to the hole and attempted to straddle it as best I could with minimal success. The floor around the hole was tile and rather slippery so I was consumed with fear that I would slip and fall on the damp floor, ruining my skirt. Somehow, I managed to relieve myself, get over to the wall and retrieve my shoes and stockings without mishap. I noticed one small bench outside the stall, so I sat on it while I replaced my pantyhose and shoes. There was also a sink in the outer chamber where I could wash my hands. I did so, straightened my suit and made my way back down the hall to the conference room.

I was still in shock when I returned to the conference room. Everyone turned when I entered the room and I could feel my face flush with embarrassment. The seminar continued and I finally relaxed as I listened to some of the experiences we would be enjoying in the weeks ahead. At about 12:30 another group of uniformed young women invaded our inner sanctum. This time they were pushing carts containing what appeared to be beautiful wooden jewelry boxes. The young women placed a box on each of our desks and then parked the carts neatly at the rear of the room.

Before they left the room, one of the young ladies approached me. I realized at once that she was the one who had given me directions to the rest room. She knelt down next to me and I saw tears in her beautiful almond eyes.

"Please forgive, gracious lady. I send you to Japanese rest room by mistake. I should send you to one for foreign dignitaries. I so sorry! I am new here and I forget there is difference. Please accept apology. I show you where to go next time when I come back for lunch box. Okay?" She rose and headed for the door before I could answer.

I examined the beautiful cherry wood box in front of me. It was about a foot wide and nine or 10 inches tall. It had carved doors on the front with hand painted inlaid flowers on them. I opened the doors with delicate wooden handles and found seven drawers inside of varying dimensions. There was a wide, thin drawer at the bottom, and it contained a soft linen napkin, a pair of ivory chopsticks and a tiny tin of wasabi paste. As I peeked into each of the other six drawers, I discovered various food items that made up this exquisite lunch. One drawer held delicately flavored rice topped with vegetables. Another drawer had several kinds of fish and still another, what appeared to be tempura. Each drawer was a container of delight and I enjoyed every morsel. Jack and Ken looked a bit non-plussed at this delicate assembly of food items but eventually seemed to get the hang of it. After all, we were in Japan now.

When the young ladies returned to claim the empty lunch boxes, the one who had spoken to me came over again.

"I so sorry about error I make. Please forgive. May I show you proper rest room now?" she inquired with a soulful expression.

"Of course," I answered and stood up to follow her. She led me in a different direction altogether, and at the end of another hall she pointed to a door that said *Ladies* in English on the door. I thanked her profusely and assured her she was forgiven. I pushed open the door and was amazed to find myself in one of the most elegant rest rooms I had ever seen. Truly, someone at Hitachi did understand the meaning of Western culture. How could they not adopt this as their own I wondered?

Chapter 34

The seminar continued until late afternoon when we were dismissed to tackle the subway one more time in an effort to return to our hotel. Our guide informed us that there would be a formal dinner tonight for all attendees before we left tomorrow for a visit to the castings plant at Yasugi. This trip to the northern part of the island would be a long journey by train and we would spend two nights there, staying in a small local hotel in the vicinity of the foundry. It was suggested that we pack a small bag for this trip and leave the remainder of our clothing in our rooms in Tokyo. I was excited at the prospect of traveling by train to a new part of Japan, especially to Yasugi where much of the product I handled was made.

I was better prepared for my subway ride this time, and when the "paddle man" came along, I pushed my way into the center of the car and avoided the prod of his weapon against my back. It was less crowded this time than this morning, I noticed – probably because so many Japanese men worked late at the office as was their custom. Many business deals were concluded far into the evening in the local bars that filled the high-rise buildings in the *Ginza*, I was told. In these small establishments men purchased bottles of liquor, had their names put on them and kept them there to be used whenever they came to do business. Each man had his own bottle with his preferred brand and when it was consumed entirely, it was immediately replaced with another.

Our formal Hitachi dinner was at a local steak house which was known for its Kobe beef. Although the menu was in Japanese I could convert the Yen prices into dollars. I was so startled at the results of my computations that I almost lost my appetite. The first steak on the menu was $150 but no one at the table seemed to bat an eye. Apparently this was not the exception but the norm. How could people afford to live in this country I wondered?

As I continued to peruse the menu, I realized that food was not uppermost in the minds of the diners in our party. Drink orders were being shouted from one end of the table to the other and suddenly I was called upon to order.

Ken whispered in my ear, "They start with beer, followed by Saki, and then they pour the Scotch. They will expect you to keep up Joansan so consider yourself forewarned." This comment was punctuated by what passed for a giggle and I knew I was potentially in deep trouble.

"I'll handle it," I shot back and ordered a beer. Several of the men cheered, and I know I was blushing. The beers were delivered to the table and before I could even drink half of mine, the waiter was behind me with a tray of Saki glasses. More cheering. I downed the beer and picked up the Saki glass that was in front of me. It was ceramic – tall and thin and rather warm to the touch. I took a sip. When I tell you I could not speak, I am not kidding. I thought I would never speak again. The clear liquid snaked down my throat and stung my insides like an asp escaped from an Egyptian queen. The room echoed with shouts of *Kampai* as the men downed their glasses. I remained speechless and as soon as I could, I excused myself and took me and my glass to the ladies room. I rushed into the first stall I saw and poured the contents into the toilet. I went to the sink and filled my cupped hands with water and drank as much as I could I examined my face in the mirror and saw that I was indeed in a state of permanent blush. I refreshed my hair and makeup, adding some lipstick to my mouth and headed back to the table.

No one stood up at my return, thank God! They were on their second glass of scotch and already too drunk to notice if I were there or not. This was my saving grace because now they would not know if I were drinking or watering the potted plants. I would just keep saying *Kampai* and pouring the contents of my glass in Jack or Ken's or in any potted palm I could find handy. After an hour or two had passed someone decided to order dinner. I ordered the steak I wanted by looking at the picture and pointing at it for the benefit of the waiter. The meal was delicious, but I am convinced that I was the only one that could really appreciate it. The drinks kept flowing even though the food had been served. Ken and Jack were more sheets to the wind than I care to recount and I don't think there was one sober Japanese at the table. Nevertheless, the food disappeared just like the liquor and everyone seemed to have a wonderful time. We all returned to the hotel in a private bus, and I must confess it was worse than the subway experience. – like being jammed into a conveyance with a bunch of drunken, unruly boy scouts. Being the only woman in the group was definitely a disadvantage. It rapidly became a matter of survival as I fended off proposals for various ways to continue the frivolity. I for one was going nowhere but straight to my room for what was left of a good night's sleep.

I awoke with a clear head but I think I was the only one not encumbered by a hangover of rather large proportions. We had our usual breakfast in the hotel and then were taken by mini-bus to the train station. I didn't even see Ken or Jack until we got on the bus. Both were asleep in their seats in the very rear of the bus. I opted to sit up front so I could have a better view of the streets as we drove to the station.

"Have you ever been on a bullet train?" the man next to me inquired.

"No," I answered. "Does it go pretty fast?"

"It is the fastest train in the world," he answered. "We will be in Yasugi in no time."

Another first, I thought to myself. I'm glad I'm not too hung over to enjoy the ride. When we arrived at the station we were told the train was already there and we could board immediately. We were led to the platform where a sleek silver train awaited. We boarded and our adventure began at once. A long, low whistle blew twice and the train started to move. We went into a tunnel and began to pick up speed almost as soon as we exited the other side. Before I could say another word, the train was speeding along the tracks. It was going so fast that I could barely see the scenery going by. My seat mate was true to his word. We reached Yasugi in less than two hours. After checking his watch, he smiled and announced that we had travelled at a rate of 150 miles an hour. I was definitely impressed and said so.

We were invited immediately into the foundry which covered the land in front of us as far as the eye could see. Huge is the word that comes to mind. The buildings had a soft orange glow and the sound of the great turbines was deafening. We were brought to a special room where we were asked to don "clean suits" over our clothes before being allowed on the floor. These garments consisted of oversized coveralls, a jacket with long sleeves, resembling a doctor's coat, and a small cap to cover our hair. Fortunately mine was quite short – not much longer than the men's. Dutifully garbed we left the room and, after walking down a long hall and through huge double doors, we found ourselves on the floor of the foundry itself. The noise that filled the space was intimidating and the immense ovens which baked the castings dominated the walls in front of us. We watched gigantic auto parts roll down an assembly line through a huge pit of fire and end up in one of the massive ovens. Further on we saw castings belching out of smaller ovens and being doused with liquid, creating clouds of steam in their wake. All in all it was a mystical and exciting process and our guide, who spoke rather good English, explained each detail of the journey. I confess I was totally fascinated, although I did not always understand each facet of the process.

We broke for lunch about one o'clock and were herded into the cafeteria where we reclined on long benches set up much like picnic tables. There were many workers in this room all sitting at the same type of benches.

"This is the second lunch shift," our guide informed us. "There will be two more after this one and all will receive the same food. Please take a tray from the rack, form a line at the counter and you will be given your food."

Ken and Jack stood up immediately and headed for the rack of trays. They must be hungry, I thought, since they missed out on breakfast. I followed behind and took my tray in turn.

A man dressed all in white filled my tray as soon as I placed it on the counter. I did not take time to consider the contents but made my way back to the bench. After I sat down I examined the food more closely. The plate was large and consisted of compartments. Each indentation contained a different food – in the same manner as the jewelry box lunches at the corporate office. There was a large portion of rice in the center surrounded by various types of fish and vegetables. There was no bread and the beverage was a large glass of what appeared to be green tea. I brought a forkful of one of the fish to my lips and was greeted with a subtle taste of sweet – sesame I decided and moved my fork on to another section. Each one had a different flavor and the vegetables were prepared tempura-style. As with the fancier lunch, the food was wholesome and delicious. No wonder they all stay slim and healthy, I thought. I finished every morsel and downed the glass of green tea. After an hour had passed our guide stood up and motioned us to follow him to another section of the foundry where the huge mill rolls were produced. We followed him dutifully and were once again in awe of the power of what was going on around us. I could not help but notice how clean the areas were as we approached each phase of the foundry operation, and yet we were almost constantly engulfed in smoke and heat and the melting and molding of masses of iron material. Cleanliness was very much a part of the process and again, I was very impressed.

As they herded us into a mini-bus to return to our hotel, I wondered if another dinner like last night was in the offing. I was informed that dinner would be a quieter affair in our hotel dining room and would commence at seven o'clock. Their idea of quiet was still pretty raucous for my taste but as the only woman I was determined to keep a low profile without being a prude. I got through the evening unscathed and enjoyed some outstanding sushi in the bargain. My Japanese companions were most impressed that I even knew what sushi was and even more impressed when they realized how much I enjoyed one of their favorite foods.

The next morning we boarded the train again and continued on our journey to Kobe, home of the steel mills. Of all the places we visited, the most interesting for me were these world famous steel mils. One of the first things I learned when I joined Hitachi Metals America was that 95% of the world's razor blade steel was made by Hitachi. On top of this fact no razor blade steel was made in the USA at all. The other 5% was split between Sweden and Germany. I had visited Bethlehem Steel in Baltimore with Peter and so I was totally unprepared for the steel mills outside of the port city of Kobe. They were so clean and so many of the procedures were carried out by alien beings called robots – huge robots at that.

As with the foundry in Yasugi we were asked to don clean suits but these were even more complex. You would think we were astronauts going on a moon mission. We were completely covered from head to foot, including helmets that completely covered our heads and faces. The suits were like one piece pajamas with feet in them so there was no exposure between ankles and feet. We even had to wear gloves on both hands. The floors we walked on as we entered the mill itself appeared to be clean enough to eat off of. We all wore badges around our necks as well to identify us as we walked from section to section where the giant robots were busy rolling out thin sheets of steel like silver tissue paper. The whole scene was awesome! We spent two very educational days in Kobe and then continued on up the coast to the foundry where they make the Rolling Mills which are the huge rolls that are used in the manufacture of many auto parts and also in the steel mills.

By the end of the second week the Americans in the group were dying for some red meat. Fish was about all we had eaten for the past two weeks other than the night in the steak house, so when we arrived back in Tokyo, we took off running into the *Ginza* and through the golden arches to – you guessed it -- MacDonald's. "Big Macs all around," shouted Ken. Nobody argued. We literally gorged ourselves on burgers, fries and milkshakes – like parched nomads finding an oasis.

Chapter 35

⌘

The last week of our cultural journey was perhaps the most enlightening. We traveled by train and bus to reach a retreat house owned by Hitachi and nestled at the foot of Mt. Fuji. My first view of this ethereal place was in late afternoon when the sky was beginning to turn orange as the sun slid down behind the magnificent mountain. It was reminiscent of a picture postcard I recalled receiving from one of our young executives who had returned to Japan recently after his stint in the USA was complete.

The eighteen members of our group were to be the only guests in this amazing edifice. It was built rather like a Swiss Chalet with windows all around a large tower-like structure at its apex. It seemed to snuggle into the arms of the mountain like a child hugging a huge woolly dog. We entered the front door and were directed to the second floor by an elderly man dressed in, what I can only describe, as Japanese pajamas. He introduced himself as Mr. Suzuki. We climbed a circular staircase to the upper floor. Our host bowed and then pointed to a large room on the right filled with *Atami* mats and small wooden cabinets lining the walls. I realized immediately that this was the normal sleeping accommodation for this retreat house which had never had a woman in residence before – until now. I hesitated.

I stepped back and let the men go past me into the room. I walked over to Mr. Suzuki and bowing touched his arm. He turned and looked at me – probably for the first time.

"Ohhhhhhh" were the only words that escaped his lips. He paused for a moment and then spoke again in very broken English. "You please wait here, Miss. I fix room for you."

I saw Jack and Ken peering out the door of the sleeping chamber grinning like Cheshire cats. "Guess you're a first, huh, Joansan?" Ken quipped. "Let us know if you need to be tucked in," added Jack.

I gave them such a devastating look, it sent them scrambling back into the room. Just then Mr. Suzuki returned. He had a young man with him and they were carrying a large *Shoji* screen and a cot. He indicated a door a bit further down the hall from the men's sleeping quarters and set down the screen and the cot. The door opened into a walk-in closet attached to a tiny bathroom. Mr. Suzuki and the young man set up the screen in such a way as to provide me with a private entrance to the closet/room which was to become my bedroom for the duration of our stay. They placed the cot inside against the far wall and added a duvet and a pillow. Japanese men don't usually blush, but I was certain that Mr. Suzuki's face was not usually so very pink in color.

I bowed slightly and muttered *Arigato* in my best Japanese and then added, "This will be just fine." He seemed to understand and smiled with relief as he bowed and walked toward the stairs. I saw there was a small cabinet inside the closet and quickly unpacked my few belongings. As I was stowing my small suitcase under the cot, I heard a voice in the hall. A well dressed Japanese gentleman was requesting our presence downstairs for an orientation. I left my room and joined my group as they proceeded down the spiral staircase.

We were guided into a rather large room with many windows and asked to take a seat. The room was full of light for so late in the day and had a comforting aura about it. There were no chairs in the room, but the floor was covered with large, comfortable-looking cushions. We each selected a cushion and lowered ourselves onto the floor. I had slacks on so was able to sit cross-legged on the cushion just as most of the men did. The gentleman who served as our guide was standing at the front of the room. There was a small raised dais there also equipped with a cushion. As soon as everyone was seated, he introduced himself and lowered his small frame onto the cushion. He surveyed the group in front of him with quiet interest and glanced at me briefly. I waited but he showed no sign of alarm at seeing a woman in his audience.

"I am pleased to welcome you all here," he said after bowing gracefully from the waist. He then began to speak in Japanese. "I will address you in both languages the first day of our meeting," he advised. "After that time, I will speak mainly in English. If some of your counterparts have difficulty understanding, I expect you to use any means in your power to help them to understand. Is that clear?" We all nodded and he continued.

"There are twelve countries represented here this week. In only three of these countries is English the language of choice. In all but two English is taught as a mandatory second language. Therefore, please make every effort to help those whose English skills are not as good as yours. I also expect many of you to become more fluent in some of the basic Japanese phrases, and I will be available to assist in this endeavor." We all nodded again.

We will enjoy a light dinner this evening and then you will be free to wander the grounds or visit other parts of the building as you wish. We have a dining room, a library and a small gymnasium on this floor for your use. We want you to feel at home. We will begin our day early tomorrow morning with a wakeup call at 7:00 a.m. I know you were told to bring comfortable clothing for this trip – business attire is not required. That is because, as you see, we sit on the floor for our meetings and, as you will find tomorrow, we start every morning outside with group exercise. This is the way all Japanese companies start their day and we hope you too will comply with our program of activity. Following the group exercise, those who feel up to it, will jog on the track at the foot of our mountain. We feel it is a most stimulating way to start the day and hope that you will choose to join in this activity. Breakfast will be served in the dining room following these activities. Let us now adjourn to the dining room for dinner.

The alarm went off at 7:00 a.m. as promised in the form of a subtle gong-like sound from the lower reaches of the building. I raised myself up on one elbow and tried to adjust to the dim light in my tiny space. Fortunately, the bathroom at the rear of the closet had a small window in the back wall which allowed some light to filter into the room adjacent to it where I was sleeping. I could hear a cacophony of sound from across the hall and knew it must be emanating from the men's dormitory. After all, seventeen men all in one room together had to create some serious male bonding sounds. I grabbed my kimono and stuck my head out into the hall. I retreated almost immediately when I realized that my fellow attendees were all heading for the communal bathroom down the hall, and all were wearing nothing but their skivvies. This being the only woman in the group was getting to be more of a challenge every day.

I raced back into the bowels of my cubbyhole and determined a shower was not going to be part of my usual ablutions today. I utilized the tiny bathroom to take a sponge bath and ready myself for the day ahead. I put on a pair of jogging pants, a t-shirt and a jacket, and shoved my feet into socks and sneakers. I dabbed some pressed powder on my slightly blushing cheeks, added a dab of lip gloss and headed for the stairs. Jack and Ken were just coming down the hall as I hit the top step. They waved and I returned the salute with a grin. When we got outside Mr. Suzuki was waiting for us and we lined up on the grass where he indicated. Within minutes he began a calisthenics routine and did not even stop to breathe for at least fifteen minutes. He then asked us to recline on the grass and we went through a series of stretches that utilized parts of my body that I didn't know existed. *Boy, was I out of shape.*

After a full twenty minutes of exercise, Mr. Suzuki announced that we would take a break for five minutes before running around the track.

I looked from Ken to Jack and began shaking my head. There was no way I was going to go jogging. Mr. Suzuki had other ideas, however, and ten minutes later I was on the track with the rest of the gang. I asked him if I could do brisk walking instead of jogging and, after looking me up and down and realizing that I was a 40-something woman, he acquiesced. I made it halfway around and then cut across the oval and headed for the gym. Things got even more interesting after breakfast. We had our first cultural exchange meeting. We broke into four groups – two with four people each and two with five. Mr. Suzuki carefully mixed us up so that every group had English speaking members as well as Japanese. We were given scenarios to discuss and problems to solve associated with them. Trying to understand and make ourselves understood was very challenging. Each group had a different scenario and accompanying problem to solve. The idea was to discuss, vote on, then hopefully, agree on our solution. Each group selected a spokesperson who would present the problem and its ultimate solution.

Presenting these problems and solutions took the rest of the morning and only two of the groups had presented before it was time for lunch. Mr. Suzuki looked more than a little harried as he led us into the dining room. I sat with Jack and Ken and we compared notes as each of us was in a different group. Jack's group had presented already, but Ken and I still had to face this in the afternoon. Jack said that the Japanese group member was anxious to be the presenter so that made it a little easier. He had to admit that he was not sure about the result. One member of his group was from France and spoke pretty good English. One was from Spain and his accent was very heavy, and one was from Taiwan. The one from Japan had difficulty understanding both of them. He advised us to speak very slowly and clearly and ask our Japanese or non-English speaking members if they understood before going on with the discussion.

I got through the remainder of the afternoon and when our turn came to present, I was feeling pretty good about my little group. Our German member was chosen to present. His English was excellent and he also had a lot of practice with Japanese so it went very well. We got a round of applause from our compatriots and Mr. Suzuki was smiling broadly. After this, it got a little easier every day, and before the week was over, we were all feeling pretty good about ourselves. The camaraderie was high and all the members were learning to mingle with each other and find common grounds for discussion. I began to realize the real value of what we were doing.

On the last afternoon of our stay Mr. Suzuki took us up yet another flight of stairs into the tower section of the building. The room we entered was quite small and se we experienced rather close quarters as we entered and settled onto our cushions. This was the Meditation Chamber, he advised, and although we were all of different belief systems we would come here together as a group to meditate.

"You each have your own idea of a higher power," he explained in English and then in Japanese, "so I want each of you, in your own way, to silently address that thought and meditate on it for a few moments. No words will be spoken in this room until I inform you that we are ready to leave. You will hear soft music playing in the background and you may even experience a sense of smell that is unfamiliar to you. Please enjoy these amenities and continue with your meditation until you once again hear the sound of my voice."

Time became meaningless in this space and I felt my body and mind relax in a way I had never experienced before, even in church. The music was from an unfamiliar instrument; reminiscent of a harp and the strange aroma was flower-like but yet not really floral. I felt my eyes close and my heart beat slow. A sense of peace and complete relaxation permeated my being as I let my mind wander. I thought of the beautiful mountain outside, of the amazing variety of temperaments and cultural backgrounds that were united in this small room. I felt grateful for this spiritual experience and knew that my higher power was indeed with me today.

Mr. Suzuki's voice broke the silence after what seemed like a very long time. After consulting the watch on my wrist I was surprised to note that only fifteen minutes had passed.

We all rose slowly to our feet and looked around at each other. No one spoke or felt the need to. The silence was comforting, like a warm blanket on a cold morning. We followed Mr. Suzuki back down stairs to the first floor and, without being told, we all passed through the large double doors and went outside into the garden. The sun shone brightly over Mt. Fuji and we could clearly see the white snow that covered the giant dome. Mr. Suzuki joined us momentarily and took a seat on one of the benches in the middle of the garden.

"The meditation exercise you just experienced is the last group activity of your visit here," he said softly. "I hope you found it a fitting way to end your stay in Japan. We have accomplished much during these past weeks, and I hope the experience was as stimulating for you as it was for me. Tomorrow you will board the train to return to Tokyo and two days hence you will all be back in your own countries. Although this visit will become just a memory, I hope you will all take something home with you that you did not have when you arrived. Good luck to all of you and I hope you will return to our country some time in the future."

We all stood and expressed our thanks with a round of applause followed by a shaking of hands. No one was anxious to break the mood and proceed down to the dining room for what we knew would be our last dinner in this magical place.

Chapter 36

It was good to be home and I buckled down to my usual busy routine very quickly. The ensuing months passed without incident and I enjoyed every moment of my working days. I thought often about the trip to Japan and felt more at ease with my Japanese compatriots than I had before. There was no doubt in my mind that the experience had made me a better manager.

One day Peter was called into a meeting with the President, Mr. Hiromoto and the accounting department. When he came out of the meeting several hours later, he looked a bit perplexed. He called me into his office.

"We're opening a new office in Baltimore and setting up a private truck fleet to handle all our freight that comes into that port. It will be our job to set up that fleet and to find a building to house it in. I'll be spending a lot of time in Baltimore getting things set up and you will be in charge of the operation up here till I get back. Think you can handle that?"

I was temporarily rendered speechless. When I found my voice, I answered with enthusiasm.

"Of course I can. You taught me everything you know and the rest I learned at the Traffic Academy. I've continued to take transportation courses at the local community college to keep up on everything so I'm as ready as I'll ever be. Besides, you're not going to the North Pole. You'll be available for me to talk to if I need help, won't you?"

Peter smiled. "Pretty confident, huh? I guess I did a pretty good job of turning you into the first woman traffic manager. I think you'll be okay – in fact, I'm sure of it. I will need your help in setting up the paper work between offices and some of the procedures we'll need to keep control of the operation. As soon as I hire a manager for the Baltimore operation, I will only have to fly down there once a month to keep the lines of communication open, but until then I will have to stay there and get the operation up and running. It may take a few weeks to find the right man for the job, but I'll get on it right away," he assured me.

These words turned out to be lethal. The man Peter hired did not work out. After only a few months it was evident that our fleet operation was in trouble. As soon as Peter left the Baltimore site, all hell broke loose. The manager became a despot, ruling the operation by his rules not Hitachi's. He checked no logs, kept no records of fuel consumption and generally kept no legible record of transactions. He completely ignored all of Peter's instructions and just did his own thing. The filing system was non-existent and the drivers were about to mutiny.

Peter returned from Baltimore after a call from our lead driver. When he discovered what was going on, or rather not going on, he fired the man on the spot and returned to New York to initiate a solution to our immediate problem.

He came into the office early Thursday morning, right from the airport. He was pacing as he shouted for me to come to his office on the double – not his usual habit.

"Pack your bags; you're leaving for Baltimore on Monday."

"Who me? Are you crazy? I don't know anything about trucks."

"You've been laying the groundwork to set up the operation and working with the leasing companies for more than three months now. How much more do you need to know?"

I looked at my boss incredulous. Negotiating contracts did not a trucking company manager make. He had to be out of his mind. The drivers would hate me. They would never accept a woman as their boss, especially one as ignorant about the art of truck driving as I was.

"You can hire another guy to be manager. There're lots of them in Baltimore."

"He'll only turn out to be another little king," Peter said, "and I'll have to fire him just like I did the last one. You're a smart girl; you learn fast. I've taught you everything I know about transportation and the rest you can get at school or you can pick up from the drivers."

Oh sure, I thought to myself. The drivers will love that – teaching a dumb woman about driving a truck and hauling freight to every God forsaken outback from here to the Mississippi.

"I tell you what," Peter finally agreed. "I'll give you three months to try it out. If you absolutely hate it at the end of that time, I'll bring you back to New York."

"Do you promise?"

"I promise," he conceded. "I'll make the trip down with you on Monday just to tell the guys and give you some moral support. By the way, three new trucks have been ordered and will be coming in on Friday. You'll have to check them out to be sure they meet all the specifications. It's a good way to get your feet wet."

"Wet, shmet," I grumbled. You're throwing me to the lions and you don't even have a conscience about it."

"Cool down, Joan," was his reply. "You've never let me down yet."

On Monday we took a ten-seater prop out of Westchester Airport and arrived in Baltimore about noon. We drove to the rented warehouse where the company had set up their new private truck fleet. We walked in the door of a large dismal warehouse, and I all I could see was one dirty desk, two rusty filing cabinets and crates of iron castings stacked half way to the ceiling. I heard a roar behind me and barely got out of the way before a bright yellow fork lift screeched to a halt at the door.

"Hiya, boss," said the fork lift driver, a short, squat, burly guy with thick black hair down to his shoulders. "Where's the new guy? From the papers I got it seems like his name is John Breen or somethin' like that."

"I've got a surprise for you, Mario," Peter answered with a grin. "The new guy is right here. Meet Joan, Mario, not John. Her name is Joan and she's the new manager."

Mario went white, if that is possible for a first generation Italian from the south of Italy. "A girl! You hired a friggin' girl to manage this place?"

I stepped forward, feeling rather awkward in my navy blue suit and three inch heels. "I'm very pleased to meet you, Mario, and I hope we'll be able to work together.

He looked at me with utter astonishment. "Yeah, yeah," he said. "Sure." He began to grin and I thought any minute he would burst out laughing. He looked at Peter and scratched his chin.

"Most of the guys are at the pier right now," he said. "They should be coming back in about two o'clock. With a wave and a smile he hopped back on his fork lift and headed out into the bowels of the warehouse. I looked at Peter and shrugged. This was not going to be the piece of cake he promised me—not at all.

"Let's go to lunch" Peter suggested. "It'll all look better after some good food."

When we returned from lunch the drivers were all waiting in the dispatch room. I looked with wonder at the big red and white trucks and gleaming aluminum trailers parked in neat rows in the back of the warehouse. They were so huge and shiny with the company logo emblazoned on the doors. I felt a jolt of pride as I looked at them.

Peter wasted no time. "Gentlemen, I'd like to introduce Joan Greene, your new Fleet Manager. She's a little new to trucking but spent months helping to set up this operation. I'm sure you'll give her all the support you can and together you'll make a great team. The company is counting on you to give our customers the best service you can, and Joan is here to see that you do."

He stepped back, folded his arms across his chest, and waited for a reaction. The first response – a *hrmph* deep in the throat – was from a six foot tall black man who looked to weigh about 250lbs. He stepped forward, hands on hips, and surveyed us both with narrowed eyes.

"Well, boss, I'll personally see to the safety of this little lady. No one is gonna give her any unnecessary trouble or they'll have me to answer to."

I smiled and stepped forward to shake the hand of this giant who just offered to be my protector. "And what is your name, sir?"

"Daniel, Daniel Smith, Maam, and I is pleased to make your acquaintance."

"For a few minutes no one else said a word. Six other drivers, all white and well built, just stood there gaping at me.

Finally a handsome man of about thirty five, clean cut, with a uniform that appeared to be newly pressed said, "I'm Jack Phillips, number one driver. That means I have the most seniority so I get first choice on all runs. I'll give you all the help I can, and I'm sure I speak for the rest of the guys too." He looked around at the other drivers and spoke with very little conviction but at least he wasn't hostile.

The five other drivers just stood there. It was obvious to me that they were very uncomfortable. Peter broke the silence and introduced each man to me in turn. "One or two are missing, Joan. They're on the road making deliveries. You'll meet them tomorrow."

"I'm gonna take Ms. Greene to her hotel and then head out to the airport. She'll be here at 8:00 a.m. tomorrow, boys, and then you can all get acquainted. Jack, I'm leaving you in charge till then. Don't let the place burn down and good luck to all of you."

He grabbed me by the elbow and steered me toward the door.

Chapter 37

Tuesday morning came early. I walked into the warehouse at 8:00 a.m. clad in blue jeans and boots, and headed right for the dispatch room.

"Morning, gentlemen," I chirped, trying to hide my abject terror. "I guess it's time to go to work. I know I'm a shock to some of you and a disappointment to most of you, but the truth of the matter is you are stuck with me. I admit I know nothing about driving a truck or checking the specs of one. What I do know is how to route freight and obey the laws governing that move. I also know what the company expects and how to give them what they want. So--- I want to learn what I don't know and I hope you will teach me."

I then addressed my number one driver. "Jack, I'm going to ask you to come inside for three or four weeks and work with me. I need your expertise to teach me about the trucks and handling the freight and I'll pay you top road mileage for your time. How 'bout it? Is it a deal?"

Jack stepped forward and after studying me for a moment, answered. "I'm willing to come inside for a few weeks." "My wife will be thrilled to have me home every night."

He turned around to the other drivers. "She's right, guys. We're stuck with each other so let's make the best of it. Warm up those rigs and get ready to get the rest of our freight off the pier." They nodded in unison and headed out to their trucks. I could hear them muttering among themselves.

"Mornin', Ms. Mother Trucker." The soft voice of Daniel Smith reached my ears and I didn't know whether to laugh or cry.

"You better watch how you say that, Daniel," I laughed or I might think you're makin' fun of me."

"No Maam," said Daniel. "I's just funnin' you. I just never heard tell of a woman runnin' a truck fleet bafore."

"Well, there's always a first time," I retorted. "You can call me Miss Joan from now on and we'll get along fine."

" Okay, Miss Joan. But you should use Mother Trucker for your CB handle once you learn to drive."

"Learn to drive??? I exclaimed. Are you serious?"

"I sure am," was his immediate answer. "How you gonna tell guys what to do if you can't do it youself?"

I paused in reflection and then looked Daniel straight in the eye. "And do you propose to teach me?"

"Not me, boss, but Paul Frye will do it if you ask him real nice." He grinned. "He's the teacher type and has lots of patience. He used to teach drivin' at a school down town. Ask him, Miss Joan. I know he'll say yes. Just ask him."

Now it was my turn to grin. "Okay, Daniel, I'll ask Paul. I think you're right. I have to learn to drive or the men will never have any respect for me. I'm not only going to learn to drive, but I'm going to go on the road with every driver and make deliveries to all our customers. But first, I'm going to learn about the trucks and the logs and all that stuff from Jack. I have four weeks to become a fleet manager and I'm gonna start right now."

"I believe you will, Miss Joan," said Daniel as he ambled out of the office heading for his Mack Truck parked in the back. "I'm off to the pier now. See ya'll later."

"Wait a minute, Daniel," I said. "Which one is Paul Frye?"

"He's the tall blond getting' into the International Harvester, Miss Joan. C'mon out in the yard and I'll introduce you."

I followed Daniel into the yard. He led me to the door of the biggest truck I had ever seen close up. The door was open and the driver was settling himself behind the wheel. He leaned out the window and smiled at us.

"What's up Daniel? Aren't you goin' down to the pier with us? We've still got a bunch of freight to get off the Toby Maru."

"I'm a comin', Paul. Just wanted to introduce you to our new boss. She didn't get a chance to meet you yesterday when Peter was here." He turned and waved me toward the door of the truck.

"Hi," I said. "You're Paul Frye and you used to teach driving. Is that right?"

"Yes, Maam, it is," answered the good looking blond, studying me hard.

"Well," I stammered, I have a proposition for you. Please come into the office after you get back from the pier. I'd like to talk to you – in private," I added.

"I hope I haven't gotten off on the wrong foot already, Maam," he said looking rather worried and pushing back the shock of blond hair threatening to cover his left eye.

"No indeed, Mr. Frye. There are some things I need to learn and you're just the one to teach me. See you later," and I walked away amazed at my own bravado.

I went back inside the warehouse and suddenly remembered that we were not the only tenants there. An attractive young woman was standing by the water cooler and looked up and smiled as I entered.

"Hi. I'm Patti," she said. "I'm the dispatcher/secretary for Time, DC. We're in the other half of this building so I guess we'll be seeing a lot of each other."

"I smiled back and extended my hand. "I'm pleased to meet you, Patti. I'm Joan Greene, the new fleet manager here. I must say it's a pleasure to see another woman working in this crazy business. I hope we can be friends; I could sure use one about now."

"I'm sure we will be, Joan. If you have any problems I can help with, don't hesitate to ask. We kinda help each other around here. We're not in competition 'cause you deliver to your own customers and we compete with the other truckers for freight so we're one big happy family. We do help you get freight off the pier now and then, if you need us and we're available, so we will be working together sometimes. Just take it slow and I'll see you at lunch time."

Just knowing there was another woman in the house made me feel a bit better already. I set to work trying to make order out of chaos in the tiny room that served as an office/dispatch room. I soon discovered what Peter meant about the former manager. The top drawer of the desk was filled with loose fuel tickets and various unpaid invoices. Drivers' used log books were in a pile on the floor. I picked one up and began to study it. No mileage had been computed and none of the pages appeared to be audited or approved by anyone. I had studied the log rules at the Academy and knew this was a serious error. This is where I would start getting the Fleet in shape and then I would take it one step at a time. How could we determine a profit if we didn't know what kind of mileage we were getting? It appeared that the former manager did nothing but dispatch and get freight delivered. The profit and loss in these transactions apparently were not in his realm of interest. No wonder Peter fired him. At least this was one part of the business I knew about.

Peter had told me I would be getting a computer delivered to me within a few weeks and when it arrived, I was to set up all the inventory records for the warehouse. This was a terrifying thought as I had never used a computer in my life. I decided then and there to register for computer classes right away, before the monster arrived, so I would have some idea where to start. I didn't even know how to turn one on much less operate it. I called the local community college and arranged to take classes at night starting the very next week. Fortunately, I had good friends in the New York Office who I would be working with to accomplish this task. Roy Milano in corporate would be a big help to me in devising programs to keep the records I was responsible for. I also had to learn email which was a brand new experience for me. I realized immediately that I had my work cut out for me, but somehow, even then, I knew in my gut that the effort would be worth it. This was definitely going to be an adventure.

Peter had booked me into a local residence hotel downtown for the next few months until I got settled and had time to decide if Baltimore was where I wanted to take up residence. I had driven my car down to Baltimore one weekend and felt comfortable parking it in the hotel garage each night. There was an entrance into the hotel from the garage so I didn't have to go back out on the street to get to my room. It was not fancy but it was clean and comfortable and included a small Pullman kitchen so I could do some minimal cooking if I chose. It would suit me fine for the time being and I set about trying to make it feel like home.

Chapter 38

G od was definitely watching over me. In the next few months I worked eighteen hour days so had no time to feel sorry for myself or even think about my home and my breakup with Pat. I thought of him at least once a day and he still held the honor of being the love of my life. I missed my kids desperately but kept in touch by phone as often as I could.

Meanwhile, I ate, dreamt and slept trucking and the long hours were paying off. Jack did come inside as planned and he taught me more than I thought I could ever learn about trucks and freight. We received two new International Harvesters in the first week, just as Peter had warned me. Jack helped me check them out to make certain they agreed with the specifications of our orders. They were both sleepers and were painted white with our logo in red on the doors and the wind break. One was assigned to Jack and the other to Paul. Even I had to agree, they were beautiful.

After the first month I started my driving lessons with Paul. The Eastern Avenue Mall was only a few miles from the warehouse and it had an inside road that went all around the Mall – the perfect place to learn to drive. Paul began taking me on Sunday afternoons with his old Mack truck which we now used mainly at the pier. It was smaller than the Harvester, having no sleeper in the cab, and had thirteen gears instead of fourteen. I met Paul every Sunday afternoon for six weeks and then we practiced in the evenings when he wasn't on the road in the yard behind the warehouse. This is where I learned to back in trailers.

About the time the lessons were winding down, Peter arrived in Baltimore and announced that we were going to build our own HMA building. "Before I tell you about our plans, Joan, I want your decision about staying in Baltimore permanently. Originally, you will remember, I gave you three months to make up your mind. You've had a bit more time than that, and I need your answer now one way or the other."

"I'm hooked, Peter. I couldn't leave if I wanted to. I've invested so much time and energy into this operation and I want to see it succeed. I'm staying. I'll put down roots and I'm here for the long haul if you still think I can handle it."

"There was never a question in my mind," said Peter. "I knew you could do it. I just wanted you to know you could. And now I think you're ready for whatever comes."

"The new building will be the first one we own besides the corporate office. All the other offices are in rented quarters and this will be the only private truck fleet and warehouse facility in the Hitachi network. The new building will contain a warehouse to store freight, a front lobby, an office for you and an extra one for a future sales manager, a dispatch room and a lounge for the drivers."

This was exciting news except that I knew nothing about erecting a building. Peter assured me that I would only have to be responsible for overseeing the construction – to make sure they were working and keeping the project on schedule, and for the interior decoration of the offices. He knew I had been a decorator at Lord & Taylor in New York before working at HMA so he wasn't worried about that and, truth be told, neither was I – it would be fun to do the decorating of the lobby and offices. I would almost feel like a lady again.

And so two weeks later Peter returned with Mr. Hiromoto, an architect and a corporate attorney. They began looking for the perfect site to build on and finally settled on a large lot on Lombard Street opposite the CFX rail yards. This plot of land was on the outskirts of the city but only about five miles from the Baltimore Piers so was an excellent location. The president of HMA came down the following week to check out the site and within a few weeks papers were signed and construction began.

The new building was completed in five months and we were completely moved in and operational in six. Shortly after moving in, I hired a talented young woman to be our dispatcher and put on two more drivers. We had our official opening and several executives from the New York office came down to view the site and to celebrate our new venture. Freight increased into the Port of Baltimore and before I knew it we were actually making money.

My dispatcher, Diana, had been in trucking for several years and between the two of us we devised simple dispatch sheets and computer forms to check the profitability of our runs. She also introduced me to a new phase of trucking known as backhauls. This meant finding loads to fill up our empty trailers on their way home from making deliveries. In other words – getting paid for freight in both directions. This turned out to be a lot of work but well worth the effort as it provided income the company hadn't planned on and we were soon on the way to making ourselves a profitable operation. I admit it – I was very proud of the progress we had made and so was Peter. He thanked me at the end of the year by giving me a substantial raise in salary.

On top of this good news Peter announced that I should begin attending trucking conventions as a way of increasing our contacts and finding new ways to establish these backhauls we had become so proficient in. I was excited about the prospect of some domestic travel and the opportunity to meet other executives in the industry. The first one he came up with was being held in Boston three weeks hence and was dedicated to the promotion of private carriers only. It would be a three-day affair beginning on a Wednesday morning and closing on Friday after lunch and would include seminars and lots of time for networking. I had Diana book me into the hotel where it was being held and arrange for my airline tickets direct from BWI to Boston and return.

As Diana completed the transaction, I suddenly got a crazy idea. Since the conference ended just before a weekend, why not take the opportunity to visit "the other Mrs. Greene"? I had not seen my former best friend, Jean, since she and Al had been married some six years before. We still exchanged Christmas and birthday cards and an occasional note but had not been in each other's presence for some time.

I called Jean and posed my rather unorthodox plan. To my delight, she concurred and couldn't wait for us to be together. We agreed that I would call Al up at his office in Boston and tell him that I would be in town and would like to visit Jean for the weekend. I would take a cab to his office downtown and join him on the bus ride out of Boston to the Cape where he would then pick up his car and drive us to their home.

I made the call the next day. Needless to say, Al was flabbergasted. He could not believe that I actually wanted to do this. I think the shock factor was in my favor and so when he mumbled assent, I immediately agreed and the plan was made.

The convention was a great success and I not only learned a lot but made several very good contacts for future backhauls. There was so much going on each day that I had no time to worry about my upcoming trip to see Jean. I checked out of the hotel about three o'clock and had the concierge call me a taxi to go to The Royal Globe Ins. Co. across town. I knew what floor Al was on so headed straight for the elevator in the main lobby.

As the elevator door opened on the eighth floor, I saw him waiting for me with his briefcase in his hand. Apparently, I was to be allowed to go no further into the inner sanctum. I ratcheted up a smile when he stepped forward to greet me. He declined to return the greeting and instead pushed me back into the elevator. I said nothing but grinned inwardly.

"We'll get a cab to the bus station," he mumbled incoherently and took my arm as the elevator door opened.

A cab was already at the curb and Al all but pushed me inside. I said nary a word but slid over making room for him on the bench seat. He gave our destination to the driver and we pulled into the Boston traffic. There was dead silence for a full five minutes and then he spoke.

"Why are you doing this?" he asked with a trace of anger in his voice.

"Because I want to see my friend, Jean," I answered. "And she wants to see me," I added with a measure of conviction.

"Oh," was the response and silence returned. When we arrived at the station the bus was already there and loading. Al strode to the counter and purchased a ticket for me and indicated the door of the bus where we could enter. I followed his lead and thus ensued the quietest road trip I ever experienced in the company of my ex-husband.

Chapter 39

We arrived at the parking lot in Sandwich about an hour later. Not a word had come between us and I passed the time watching the scenery go by outside my window. As we left the bus, Al indicated the direction we should walk to reach his car. He opened the door for me and I settled into the front seat, prepared for further silence. Suddenly, he spoke.

"What were you doing in Boston?"

"I told you. I was at a trucking convention."

"You mean you really are in trucking?"

"Yes, I have been for some time now. Is that so hard to believe?"

"Well, yes, I guess I can't think of you in trucking. Do you like it?"

"I love it and have made it my career."

"The kids said you went to Japan."

"That's right. I just got back a few weeks ago."

"How long are you staying?"

"I plan to leave Saturday night if that's convenient. I have a flight out of Boston at 7:30."

"No problem. I'll take you to the airport about 6:00 so you'll have plenty of time to check in."

Silence returned after this brief exchange and the next thing I knew he was pulling into the driveway of a small Cape Cod-style house and Jean was opening the front door. I jumped out of the car and ran to meet her. We hugged and both of us had tears in our eyes. Al was at a complete loss to know what to do and we were both rather enjoying his discomfort. Jean invited me inside and led me to a small but attractive guest room where I would be spending the night.

Al announced that he would be taking us out to dinner and that we would be leaving in about twenty minutes. Jean and I exchanged glances and nodded in his direction. I made a quick trip to the powder room and walked back into the living room where Jean was already waiting for me. We hugged again and I repeated how very pleased I was to see her after such a long time. She seemed to share my feelings and I was looking forward to our evening together.

The situation was less awkward than I thought it would be and we actually had a very nice meal at a local favorite restaurant, The Daniel Webster Inn. Al made an effort at conversation and talked mostly about his work and also about our old friends, the Wallaces, who still lived on Cape Cod. Time passed quickly and soon we were all back at Al and Jean's. *Now what,* I thought to myself. Al answered this question almost before I thought it.

"I will be leaving you two for awhile," he said. "I am going out for a few hours and I know you would like some time to be together. Enjoy your visit and I'll see you later."

With those few words, he walked out the door and into the car and disappeared down the driveway.

Jean turned to me and smiled, "Let's have a drink."

She went into the kitchen and returned with a bottle of white wine and a corkscrew. We toasted each other with the first glass and before I knew it, she was opening a second bottle. With each glass the talk got looser and before long I knew that Jean's marriage was on the verge of collapse. She had already decided to divorce Al when she discovered that he was having an affair with a local widow – a rich one at that. She confided that she knew that's where he was right now.

"They meet at a local bar at least twice a week," she murmured conspiratorially. "She's got horses and dogs and even owns a gift shop downtown. I guess you could say he's marrying up," she giggled. "I've known about the other woman for some time now," she added.

"You shouldn't be surprised," I said. "After all, you already knew what he put me through and a leopard doesn't change his spots. At least assure me that he isn't going to get away with leaving you with nothing like he did me."

"No way, Joan. He taught me what to do when Pat and I split and I am using everything I learned. I even got him to buy me a condo in Florida and pay for it outright so I'll have no mortgage to worry about."

She giggled again and started pouring wine from the third bottle. By this time we were both pretty smashed and secrets were flowing as fast as the wine. I hadn't been this drunk in years and I was about to pack it in when the door opened and in walked the infamous Mr. Greene. It was two o'clock in the morning and there were two drunken women in his living room.

To say he was stunned is an understatement! Imagine coming home to two inebriated women but when both of them are potentially your ex-wives that has to be an eye opener. One look at us was all it took to tell him that Jean knew where he had been and she made sure that I knew also. The jig was up as the saying goes. His secret was out and it was too late to try to lie his way out of it. From where I sat it looked like Al Greene was preparing to shed yet another Mrs. Greene. I didn't know whether to laugh or cry but considering the condition I was in, the urge to laugh overtook me and that's precisely what I did.

This raucous outburst on my part triggered a similar one in Jean and a case of mass hysteria ensued. Al could bear it no more and after a few choice curse words, he headed up the stairs to the second floor of the house. Jean passed out on the couch within a few minutes of his departure and I eventually made it to the guest room and collapsed fully clothed on the bed.

We all slept a bit late in the morning and finally got together for breakfast about eleven o'clock. Jean and I both had hangovers but considered them worth it for the inspiring evening we had had the night before. We knew we would not forget our reunion for some time to come. I showered and changed after breakfast and got myself ready for the trip back to the airport. Jean went with us and so we had a little more time to spend together. I assured her that I would be available for moral support should she need me during her divorce process and she agreed to keep me advised of where she would be in Florida so we could keep in touch.

The relief on Al's face when I exited the car at the airport gate was palpable. I am sure that was a weekend he would not soon forget.

Chapter 40

Now that business was on the increase, I found I needed to add more drivers. I called our leasing company and had two more drivers in our stable before the week was out, bringing our total to eight. This meant ordering two more trucks and trailers also. By now I knew a lot more about specking out a truck and, after a consultation with Jack, was able to do this order pretty much by myself.

The two new drivers had been assigned to pier work only and the other six handled the road trips. I called them into the office separately one afternoon in an attempt to get to know them a bit better and decide if I felt comfortable sending them out with road freight in the future.

"Afternoon, Miss Joan," Doug Corman drawled and I realized he had a slight stutter. It didn't seem to bother him much and when it happened again, he just paused and continued till he got the words out. He had unkempt curly copper hair and looked to carry about 160 lbs on his lean six foot plus frame. Definitely not my type, I thought to myself.

Instead of coming over to my desk, he lounged comfortably against the door frame and studied me.

"Have a seat," I offered.

"Prefer to stand," he responded and didn't make any move toward the chair next to my desk. He kept staring.

"Any objection to pier work?" I queried.

"Not really" was his answer.

"Would you prefer to be on the road?" I continued.

"It pays more, don't it?" was the reply

"Of course," I parried

"Well then, send me out whenever you like," he said with no change of expression whatever.

"All right, Doug. I'll keep that in mind. I stood up and came around to the front of the desk. "You can go back to work now."

He grinned, ran his eyes from the top of my head to the tip of my boots, uttered what sounded like "Whoosh" and went out the door.

I went back to my desk slightly unnerved by the interview. I knew this man was younger than the other drivers and 14 years my junior besides. Most of the other men were closer to my age. He was certainly out of a different mold than most of the men. Just then the phone rang and put an end to my reverie over the virtues or lack thereof, of Douglas Corman.

It was Peter calling from New York. Now that I had agreed to stay in Baltimore, I had found an apartment and was getting ready to move. He was calling to check on the progress of my move and to make sure I had enough help to handle it. I assured him I did and would be using a company truck and driver to move my few belongings into the furnished cottage I had rented. The tiny dwelling was on a beautiful estate on the Magothy River in Ann Arundel County and would be only a fifteen or twenty minute commute to work. I had planned to move this coming weekend and both Paul and Jack had offered to help if I needed them, but my three daughters were planning to drive down from New York to give me a hand setting up my new home and I was really excited about seeing them. Another new beginning!

Chapter 41

The cottage was quiet. The sounds of silence were almost deafening. A small ray of light came through a porch window. A sliver of moon had risen over the river. Peace had come at last after an utterly exhausting day spent moving into my first real home since being transferred to Maryland.

My first home – how wonderful I thought, hugging myself and looking around at my new surroundings. The girls had left to return to their respective homes in New York after joining me in an informal dinner of Chinese food, lately delivered from the nearest takeout restaurant found in the local phone book. We had all been hungry, as evidenced by the array of half empty cartons and a few unopened fortune cookies. My daughters had been such a big help to me. They brought the last of my personal belongings with them from my New York apartment. I was very grateful as I could never have accomplished the move by myself, and besides, it was another excuse for us to spend some quality time together. It was no longer an easy task to get all of us together at one time anymore and so our mother-and-daughter get-togethers were few and far between. I felt fortunate.

I looked around at the small cozy living room with the old stone fireplace and saw empty boxes strewn everywhere. Who would have thought I had so many belongings. After all, I had been living in a small studio apartment in New York with only the barest essentials – all I managed to keep after my divorce. The furniture I did have were gifts from several of my old clients at Lord & Taylor – an old sofa bed from one and a walnut coffee table from another. These and some accessories from Lord & Taylor "roof sales" for employees had made up the bulk of my household belongings. They had served as a home for me and my daughters for several years. The girls packed the few things I wanted to keep, took anything they wanted from the leftovers and disposed of the rest before coming down.

The cottage I rented was actually a guest house adjacent to the main house of an estate known as Tree Tops. Its name came from a row of giant elm trees, sentinels that guarded both sides of the long driveway, which wound its way from the road down to the main house, set on the edge of the beautiful Magothy River. The owners were vacationing in Europe just now so I had the whole place to myself. It felt wonderful to be in such elegant surroundings, but a bit scary too I admitted to myself as I looked out of the window at the black ribbon of river.

I don't think I have ever been in such an isolated place before. Of course, I do have a few neighbors on the main road at the beginning of the driveway, and one other family living in a small summer house on the adjacent lot. I can barely see their house from my front door, the lots are so far apart, but it is a comfort to know they are there. I must go up there soon and introduce myself, I added as an afterthought.

I gathered up the half-empty cartons of egg *foo yung*, pork fried rice and wonton soup and headed for the kitchen. I put the leftovers together into two containers and placed them in my otherwise empty refrigerator. I did have a quart of milk, a small bottle of juice and a loaf of bread, thoughtfully provided by one of my daughters. A jar of instant coffee was also evident on the counter. I smiled – they know how I love my coffee. I grabbed a sponge to clean up the table after our

Chinese picnic and then decided to tackle the empty boxes cluttering up my new home. I glanced at my watch as I headed back to the living room and realized it was already ten o'clock. *No wonder I am so tired. It's been a long, long day.*

The boxes loomed ahead of me like huge blocks abandoned in the midst of a child's construction project. I decided to attempt to flatten them and then tie them together to be stored in my small storage room off the kitchen. After all, I might need them if I ever had to move again. I shoved the bundle of flattened boxes into the storeroom and headed for the bathroom. I knew I was done – done as pooped, finished for the day and totally exhausted.

Another daughter had thoughtfully unpacked the small bag containing my toothbrush, moisturizer, and other personal items. I grabbed a wash cloth and cleaned my sweaty face and dirty hands. I brushed my teeth, more out of obligation to my dental surgeon than anything else, and returned to the living room to lock the front door.

The TV and stereo equipment, cameras, and my jewelry box were still lined up in the narrow hall going from the front door off the deck into the other part of the house. The deck was a wrap-around one that encircled the front half of the cottage facing the river. It had jalousie windows floor to ceiling and was one of the things I loved most about my new home. I glanced at the small TV and other appliances and shrugged. They would wait for another day. It was a warm night so I left the jalousie windows open to let in the breeze off the river and headed for my bedroom. Sleep was all I could think of just now.

As I entered the bedroom and turned on the small bedside lamp, I notice that again one of my daughters had thoughtfully made up my bed and even laid out a nightgown for me. I threw off my clothes, donned the nightgown in one single motion and fell into bed. The cool sheets caressed my warm skin, and I fell asleep on the way to the pillow.

I sat up in bed, reacting to a noise in the bedroom. As I opened my tired eyes, I was met with a bright light which totally blinded me. I raised myself up on one elbow and was immediately aware of a sharp pain on the right side of my head. Everything went black.

My next recollection was waking up in a dark room. As my mind cleared a little, I realized I was still in my bed, but my head was pounding and I could taste blood in my mouth. I could not move but was aware of voices in the room with me. I fought the urge to cough with every bit of restraint I could muster. There was no light, but I could hear and understand some of what the voices were saying. The words were slurred, but it was obvious that there were two voices and one of them was very angry.

"This guy must be queer," the angry voice said. "There's nothin' but women's clothes in these drawers. And there's no stash either. No sign of any grass even. Looks like that stuff in the hall is all we're gonna get here."

As I listened to the angry murmurings, I realized that whoever was there thought I was a guy and probably already dead. My head was pounding so loudly I was sure they could hear it. I could feel myself choking on the blood that kept running down the back of my throat and collecting in my mouth.

Please God, please, don't let me cough. If they hear me, they will finish the job and kill me for sure. My only hope is to remain quiet until they leave and then figure out what to do.

"Poke him," I heard the angry one say; "make sure he's out."

I felt a hand come down on my shoulder and shake it. I held my breath. The hand shook me hard again, and I felt the blood rise in my mouth.

Please God, please help me. I cannot cough. If I do, I will die. Please, please help me stay quiet. I am begging you.

As I prayed, I felt the lump in my throat ease and go down. In that instant I knew my prayer had been answered. I lay motionless until I heard the kitchen door slam, followed by the sound of footsteps on the gravel drive. My head and heart were still pounding, but instinctively I knew I was safe – at least from any further assault.

I waited what seemed like many minutes before I attempted to move. I realized immediately that getting out of the bed was not going to be an easy task. I strained to rise on one elbow. I used all my strength to move my body to the edge of the bed. As my leg went over the side, my body followed and I found myself sinking onto the floor, choking on my own blood. My body was wracked with pain and coughing. As the coughing subsided I gathered my strength, drew a long breath and began to crawl toward the kitchen door. *I must get outside and find some help.* I had no idea of time or distance but was compelled to keep moving.

I managed to get through the screen door and out onto the side drive, which led to the river. It was very dark. I felt fear grip me. I could only see out of my left eye, but I looked down the drive and saw one tiny light at the very end. I headed for that light. I could feel the gravel cutting into my knees as I crawled, but I kept on. I had to get help. I knew I had only one neighbor near enough to reach and that must be where the light was coming from. I kept going, ignoring the gravel tearing at my knees and the pounding in my head. In the dark I made out the outline of a house and saw a small door on the side near the driveway. I crawled toward it. I felt the soft mesh of a screen and then a knob under my hand. Then everything went black.

The next thing I remember is waking up in a hospital room with two doctors and a nurse standing over me. As soon as I was able to hold my one eye open, I saw a man in a blue uniform at the food of the bed – a policeman I realized.

"I need to ask you a few questions, Maam," the man in blue said matter-of-factly.

"Can't this wait?" a doctor interjected. "She's got a broken nose, severe head and face contusions, including a concussion and trauma damage to her right eye."

"I just need to ask her a few questions," was the curt reply.

"All right," said the doctor grudgingly, "but make it quick. We've got work to do here. This lady is in a bad way, can't you see that?"

I only half heard his words -- broken nose, concussion, damaged eye. *Was that me he was describing?* All I knew was that my head and face ached terribly, and I could only see out of my left eye. *What had happened? How did I get here?* My mind was blank, and I was so tired. I turned in the bed to face the blue uniform, and was suddenly aware of my sore knees and feet. As I tried to consider why they hurt, I passed again into oblivion.

Chapter 42

W eeks later I learned what happened from a kind police detective assigned to my case and from my best friend, Sharon, who was nursing me back to health in her home.

Two young boys, high on drugs, cut the screen on the open jalousie window, reached in and unlocked the door, and entered my home. The boys thought the former tenant was still in residence. The tenant in question was an electronics salesman and small-time drug dealer on the side. The owners of Tree Tops had recently evicted him when his criminal activities were discovered, and that is how the cottage came to be available for rent.

The two teens, already high on drugs, broke in looking for electronic equipment to steal as well as drugs. When I sat up in bed, startled by the noise and with my short cropped hair, they thought I was him. The older boy struck me over the head with a table leg he was carrying as a weapon. The wooden leg broke over my head splitting my face from right to left. My nose, the doctor explained, was broken and pushed over onto my left cheek. I had a huge gash on the right side of my head, which went through my eye and down my cheek past my nose.

"The retina of your right eye is detached," the doctor said solemnly on my first visit to his office, "but there is hope that we can restore your sight. I have a lot of faith in the new laser surgery available at the University of Maryland Hospital. That is where we will send you when you regain your strength. Meanwhile, we called in a plastic surgeon to repair your nose and stitch up your face. You will need additional plastic surgery, but not until you are feeling much stronger.

"Give me a mirror," I interrupted. The nurse looked at me and then at the doctor. "Not just yet, Joan," he said. "Give us a few days to work our magic."

"No, I shouted. I want a mirror now."

The doctor shrugged and turned to the nurse. "Get her a mirror."

The nurse came back in a few minutes and handed me a small hand mirror. I took one look and promptly fainted. When I opened my eyes again, the doctor was holding my hand and looking down at me.

"You are very lucky to be alive, my dear. I hope you know that. If I were a religious man, I might begin to believe in miracles. That table leg they broke over your head was an inch and a half in diameter."

He left the room shaking his head and repeating the word, lucky, over and over to himself. I tried to absorb all that he had just told me as well as putting the mirror image out of my mind. I lay back on the examining table. I knew my survival was not luck, but divine intervention. God had not only heard my prayers, but had answered them. I guess He decided it just wasn't my time to go. How else could I have made it to my neighbor's porch and banged loud enough for them to hear me. My friend explained that they found me unconscious on their back stoop, called an ambulance and the police, and that's how I got to the hospital.

The other miraculous thing that occurred was explained to me by the detective assigned to my case. A man walking his dog in the middle of the night, before going to the late shift at the steel mill, saw a motorcycle parked at the Tree Tops gate and for some reason wrote down the license plate number. He called the police the next day when he saw the incident written up in the local newspaper. *Thank you, God,* was all I could think of right now. *Thank you for all those people and for giving me back my life.*

In the days that followed, I became more and more aware of the magnitude of this miracle. I had been away from the church for several years now, following my divorce. I had allowed a member of the clergy back in New York to convince me that I was no longer welcome in God's house, so I had stopped attending services.

But now, everything had changed. God had heard me and used these wonderful people as vehicles to keep me alive. There had to be a reason. I was not sure of the reason then, nor am I totally now, but I do know I must be a worthwhile human being – someone worth saving. This realization awakened all my senses and made me willing and anxious to do what I could to be worthy of this gift. I wanted to let God know how grateful I was and that his saving me had not been in vain.

Peter came to Baltimore soon after this incident occurred and assured me that he would stay and cover for me until I recovered. He convinced me that I had nothing to worry about except my recovery and I finally believed him. I was still staying with my dear friend, Sharon, but she had moved me to a farm house in Westminster where an old friend of hers lived. The house was huge and so they had plenty of room for Sharon and I and even my daughters. The girls came back down to Maryland and stayed for a long weekend. Their love and support were so important to my recovery.

Both young men were found, thanks to the diligence of the police detective assigned to my case. The eldest, who was 18 and actually did the beating, had to be extradited from Florida where he had fled after assaulting me. The younger boy was only 16 and weighed about 95 lbs. soaking wet. This was obvious when I saw him in court on the day of the trial. The jury found them both guilty and they were each sentenced to several years in prison. The younger boy got a lighter sentence due to his age and physical size and both were ordered to pay restitution.

After months of extensive plastic surgery and laser surgery to my right eye I had a new nose, a new face and most importantly, regained the sight in my eye. But more important than any of these, I had a new attitude and a new devotion to my God.

It was almost six months before I could return to work full time. Diana had worked tirelessly to keep things going and Peter commuted back and forth almost the entire time. He was more than my boss – he was a dear, dear friend. Fortunately, thanks to these two individuals and my exceptional team of drivers, the business not only survived my absence but flourished. It was so good to get back in the saddle and I vowed to work harder than ever to make up for lost time.

I was still living in Sharon's home in Dundalk as I had nowhere else to go I was anxious to be on my own again and give my dear friend her guest room back. Just before I returned to work, I went house hunting with a local realtor. I still had a partial bandage on my head from the last of the plastic surgery and looked a bit like someone getting ready for Halloween. I was making a pretty good salary now and decided I could afford to buy a house. For the first time in my life I would have a home of my own that no one could take away from me.

The realtor sent me to a community on a nearby peninsula on the Chesapeake Bay called Waters Edge. The house she had in mind was on a corner lot. The couple who were selling it had just remodeled it now that they were retiring and all their children were gone. Unfortunately, after they opened up the upstairs and made it into one huge bedroom accessed by a wrought iron spiral staircase, the wife became pregnant. A change-of-life baby made all the difference. The house was no longer suited to a couple with a new baby. Thus, they were forced to sell and for once in my life, I was in the right place at the right time.

The price was right but the mortgages at that time were at 17.5%. *Could I handle this?* I decided I could, knowing when the rates came down I would be able to refinance the property. And so I took the plunge and bought my first house. I couldn't wait to tell my brother and my kids. I was so proud of myself and so thrilled to be a real homeowner for the first time in my life.

I went a little crazy I think. I bought a whole new bedroom suite as well as furniture for the dining room and the living room. The house had new wall-to-wall carpeting, even in the kitchen and had just been painted so I was spared that expense. Even the appliances were all new so I felt I was justified in splurging a little.

The best thing about the house was its proximity to the office. I was on call 24/7 so could not live too far away and this was about a five-mile commute. Being on a separate peninsula with views of the water on all sides made it seem far away from the commercial area when it truth it was not. I was in love with my new house and set about making it a home with all the zeal I could muster.

The only drawback was my own innate fear. I had not lived alone since the incident (as I called it now) and wasn't sure how to handle the trepidation I felt at sleeping in the house alone. My girl friend had a cousin who was an ex-policeman and a security expert. He came to the house and proceeded to tell me what I needed to do to make the house totally secure. I agreed to his suggestions and before I moved in he arranged to put pins in the windows, install a security bolt on the storm cellar doors, secure a Charlie bar on my kitchen sliders and add a special deadbolt lock to my front door. My drivers insisted I keep a gun in the house as an extra precaution. They not only presented me with one but taught me how to use it. I kept it in my night table drawer next to my bed. My new big double platform bed, by the way, was set up in the back corner of my large bedroom facing the spiral staircase so if anyone came up those stairs, I would have a clear shot.

This gave me great comfort and only once did I pull the gun from the drawer. It was the last time I ever had a gun in my possession. My son, Brett, was home on leave from the Navy. He borrowed my car one night to go out with some friends. I gave him an extra key to get in so he wouldn't have to wake me. He stayed out rather late and when he came home at about two o'clock in the morning he decided to come upstairs to tell me he was home, in case I was worried. I had been dead asleep but am a light sleeper. When I heard the sound of steps on the stairs I grabbed for the gun and would have blown his head off if he had not shouted out, "It's me, Mom; it's Brett." He'll never know how close he came to being shot. That fact scared me so much that the next day I gave the gun back to the drivers and told them, "thanks, but no thanks."

Chapter 43

After Brett went back to the Naval base things quieted down. I felt pretty secure in the house now and was glad the gun was back with its owner. I got so good at driving the trucks that I could now back in trailers as good as the guys – at least the forty footers. I never did get the hang of the twenty footers somehow.

I began going on the road with each and every driver and eventually made deliveries to every one of Hitachi's customers. I saw more of this country by truck than I had seen in all my years of vacationing. It was one of the most exciting times of my life and I loved every minute of it. It nearly drove Peter crazy when he found out I could drive and when he'd call the office and Diana would inform him that I was on the road again, he would go berserk. It made me a much better manager and paid off in more ways than one with both the customers and the drivers.

I must admit there was a minor fringe benefit to my going on the road. Doug and I had become real close by now and were spending a lot of time together –much of it on the road. If he had an over-niter, I would go with him and we would get a motel room, which was the custom with our drivers on a run lasting more than a full day. We had several mini honeymoons that first year. As things got busier I was able to go on the road less and less and we had to settle for overnights at my house on weekends or whenever we could squeeze one in.

My daughters had met him and they all got along great, especially Ali. She and Doug hit it off right away. They became such good friends that when my father died in December the following year, Doug called her in New York and, unbeknownst to me, made arrangements to stay with her so he could be at the funeral to support me when I came north. I was so shocked to see him there and all dressed up in a suit and tie. I will never forget it. He was my rock during this very bad time.

Doug also took the place of the father Brett no longer had. Al had not spoken to Brett in several years by this time and made it clear he wanted no part of his son. On two occasions the parents of the sailors on board the aircraft carrier Eisenhower were invited to visit the ship and spend the day with their offspring. Air shows were provided and it was always an interesting experience. Doug attended two of these occasions with Brett and I, and it made it almost like a family affair. Brett was thrilled to have us both there and I was so grateful for his attendance.

I probably would never have broken up with Doug, despite the huge age difference which still bothered me somewhat, but when things started to get too serious. I panicked. He asked me to move in with him and I knew that was the beginning of the end. I cared for him very much but a permanent relationship was not in my plans. We got along great but intellectually we were worlds apart. It would never have worked and I knew it so I cut the cord. He did not take it well and went out of his way to avoid me for weeks after, taking all his assignments from Diana and making a wide swath around my office. It was a difficult time and I missed him a lot.

About six months after our breakup, Ryder hired a new man to be in charge of their drivers. He was a fox – tall, well built with a full head of wavy white hair and a well-cropped beard and a few years older than me. He looked like Kenny Rogers and I was smitten once again. Since we leased our drivers from them, Ben and I had to see each other quite often and those meetings became more and more frequent. I took him to Connecticut for a weekend to meet my brother and sister-in-law and Ben and Chuck hit it off like gangbusters. Then when Elyse and Kevin and the kids came to Baltimore to visit, I introduced him to them. They seemed to approve of the match and even asked me when we were getting married. I assured them we weren't, but the idea stayed in the back of my mind.

Three months later I agreed to let him move into the house with me. I had asked him early in the relationship about his marital status and he had assured me he was divorced. He told me he had a fifteen year old son who was living with his ex-wife, who, by the way, was fifteen years his junior. I was flattered that he preferred me to a younger woman and never questioned him further.

About a month after we returned from Connecticut, I came home from shopping one Saturday morning to find his so-called ex-wife and son parked in front of my house. I pulled in the driveway and went inside. I saw that Ben was standing by the car arguing with the woman at the wheel. The next thing I knew she got out of the car, pushed past him and rushed up the steps onto my back porch. I was in the kitchen putting groceries away when she slid open the sliding doors and entered the house. She screamed some obscenities at me and rushed into the living room. The next thing I knew pillows were flying across the room and books were hitting the floor where she hurled them. Ben came in behind her and tried to physically remove her from the house. They struggled and finally he dragged her kicking and screaming outside and shoved her back into the car. Their son just sat in the front seat on the passenger side and said not a word.

I was torn between fury and mortification. I went out on the back porch and demanded that she remove herself from my premises or I would call the Police. She was smart enough to heed my warning and backed out of the driveway keening and shouting curses at me and her husband as she did so.

When Ben came in I could hardly look at him. In the calmest voice I could muster, I asked him to pack his belongings and get out of my house. His only comment was, "we have been separated for three years, but she refused to sign the divorce papers. She's never showed any interest in getting back together until she found out I had moved in with you. I am so embarrassed and so very, very sorry. I never meant to hurt you; I just wanted us to be together."

I did not answer but just waited downstairs while he packed up his belongings. He left within the hour and we never spoke after that day except when we had to do business together. Not too long after that Ben was transferred out of Baltimore and we never spoke again. I was sad but soon got myself back on track. I learned a bitter lesson about trust and knew I would never make that mistake again.

I no sooner recovered from the loss of Ben in my life than another crisis arose. I had decided, after many unsuccessful attempts, to stop smoking once and for all. I was coughing most of the time and this gave me the impetus to try one more time. Johns Hopkins was offering a No Smoking Program and I made an appointment and went there full of positive resolve. They gave me a chest x-ray and a rather thorough physical exam before they dropped the bomb. The doctor announced that I had full blown emphysema and would be dead in a year if I did not quit immediately. I was stunned and terrified. They assured me it was too late for any program to be effective. I must stop smoking that day or my life would be over. I didn't think twice. I took the cigarettes from my purse, crushed the package with a vengeance and threw it into the waste basket. The head of the program suggested I see my doctor as soon as possible to begin treatment for the disease. He impressed on me that it was incurable but that it could be managed with inhalers and other forms of medication. I left his office with hope that it was not too late for me.

I called my doctor as soon as I got home and made an appointment. I also realized that breaking my long-standing habit of smoking would be one of the hardest things I had ever attempted. I had the shakes constantly and was a nervous wreck most of the time. I couldn't even sign my name clearly – Diana had to sign all the checks for me. I kept a coffee stirrer in my mouth most of the time (to break the mouth habit) and lived on Nicorette gum, a recent entry on the market to help people survive the loss of nicotine to their system. The first three weeks were hell but then it got easier every day. I still had the urge to smoke for several more months but finally that went away too. I gained thirty pounds during my non-smoking campaign but knew it was a small price to pay for saving my life. I worked hard at losing ten of those pounds but the other twenty I would have to accept as part of the new me.

Once again God took charge of my life. Within a few months rumors were coming down from the corporate office that we might be closing the warehouse. We had worked hard these past eight and a half years to succeed here in Baltimore and the Fleet was making more money than anyone had ever hoped it could, but the world was changing. Less and less Hitachi freight was being shipped into the Port of Baltimore because cars were being assembled in many cities in the United States now rather than in Japan and the castings we provided them were destined for other ports of call. Even the razor blade steel coming in from Japan was being re-routed mainly to the west coast so the need for a private fleet of trucks to deliver to customers from Baltimore was no longer necessary.

The call came one afternoon in the fall of 1990. "We're selling the warehouse, Joan, and you are being transferred back to the New York office. You will remain in Baltimore until all the equipment is sold and we have a buyer for the building but I suggest you make arrangements to sell your house and move back to New York before the end of the year. The company will pay all your moving expenses, of course, and will give you two weeks to come north and look for a place to live before the closing is final. I hope that will give you enough time."

"That will be fine, Peter," I responded, "but what will I do in New York?"

He paused. "I don't know, Joan. That will depend on the attitude of the new president. He is the one who decided to close you down and he has not announced his plans for you yet. I'll let you know as soon as I know something."

This did not make me feel too confident. I didn't think I was in danger of being unemployed, *but what in God's name was I going to do in the Corporate Office? Peter is Traffic Manager and has a capable assistant traffic manager already. All I know is traffic. What in the world will I do now? I am used to wearing jeans and boots to work and have acquired the mouth of a longshoreman. How am I going to fit it? What will a mother trucker do in a corporate environment with mostly Japanese employees? I am depressed!*

Chapter 44

I decided to make a quick trip to New York before we sold the warehouse and while we were preparing to close down our operation. HMA gave me two weeks to find a place to live and prepare to move back to the northeast and I wanted to make the most of it.

I contacted a realtor up there from Baltimore and told them to start looking for a condo in New York or Connecticut but within a half hour's driving distance from our Purchase office. I called my daughter, Elyse, and arranged to stay with her in Ossining while I looked at perspective places to live. It soon became apparent that the taxes in New York were higher than Connecticut and so I concentrated on Norwalk which was right next door to my brother's home in Darien. *It would be nice to live close to the only real family I had left, other than my kids.*

When I arrived at Elyse's I called the realtor and she was prepared to take me out looking the very next day. We looked at condos for two whole days and finally settled on one in a development known as Ledgebrook in Norwalk. It was a first floor condo, a short walk from a small pond and the swimming pool on the property. There was a lovely patio in the back with its own little garden. The bedroom was a good size and there was a second bedroom as well that I could use as a den/

guest room. It was a bit higher in price than I had planned on but the area was good with the church around the corner and the Community College just down the street, and best of all, the commute was only about twenty minutes. I managed to get a mortgage without too much trouble and found myself closing on the deal less than a month later. Hitachi approved the move and I contacted a moving company before returning to Baltimore.

Selling my house was the easiest thing of all. I found a buyer in the first week it was on the market and was able to close before I left for New York. I had paid a very small price for my little palace on the bay and got back twice what I had paid for it. Connecticut was pricey but at least this softened the blow somewhat. I hated to leave my first real home but was exited about returning to the Northeast and being close to my brother and my kids again.

We sold the warehouse and all our equipment. Saying goodbye to Diana and my dear, loyal drivers was the hardest thing I ever had to do. They had been my family for almost ten years and now we were all going our separate ways. We had a farewell crab feast at Diana's the weekend before I left for Connecticut and many tears were shed that day. We vowed to keep in touch and wished each other well but I knew in my heart I would probably never see most of them again. It was time to start another phase of my life and I hoped I was up to the task.

In the fall of 1989 I moved into 22 Ledgebrook Drive and began working in the corporate office. While I was still in Baltimore, HMA had done some re-organizing. They wanted to initiate a brand new department known as Community Relations. Several managers, including myself, applied for the position of Director of this new department. The manager who was eventually selected was Stuart Kirk, also the head of the Computer Dept. I was asked to work with him and assume the role of Community Relations Officer. This was a far cry from being the company "mother trucker" but the salary was excellent and the job description was intriguing. I would organize and facilitate groups known as Community Action Committees (CAC) first in the corporate office and then in all the branch offices across the country. I would also have an opportunity to work with my counterparts in several other Hitachi companies such as Wire and Cable in Manchester, NH and Hitachi America in nearby Tarrytown.

In addition to this I would be responsible for producing a monthly newsletter of some twelve pages that would be distributed country wide as well as to Japan, form a network with non-profit organizations in our area to determine the amount of our corporate donations, head up the Awards Dept. for retirees and establish a volunteer program that would include all our employees – both Japanese and American. What a challenge I had accepted. I had never worked with Stuart before but found that we had a lot in common – both being Gemini. He was a brilliant mentor but a bad teacher when it came to the computer. He preferred to do it himself rather than instruct, stand back and let me do it and then implement constructive criticism. It was very difficult at first as I had to learn a very elaborate software program in order to produce the newsletter and he had little patience with my complete lack of publishing knowledge. He finally agreed to let me go to the local community college to learn about the software and with a few months I was performing like a pro. I became the last word, if you will, on software publishing, the manipulation of photos and the use of color in a newsletter. I loved it! We decided to name the publication *The Circle*, and the first issue was a huge success. I was so proud of the success of my efforts and Stuart was extravagant with his praise. I loved my new job and determined to succeed in all the areas of responsibility given to me. By this time I had also relearned how to wear business suits appropriate to my position and to cleanup my trucker's mouth accordingly. The latter accomplishment was a great relief to my daughters who were beginning to fear I would corrupt the vocabulary of my grandchildren.

I began travelling to the branch offices every few months and made a host of new friends and acquaintances among Hitachi personnel. I contacted the various schools in our area and set up volunteer programs to aid them. I then contacted many of the non-profit organizations in our community and set about determining the amount of the corporate donations we would give annually based on their needs and our charitable interests. A whole new world of philanthropy and humanitarian skills was opening up to me and I enjoyed this new challenge tremendously.

Meanwhile my social life changed too. I was no longer surrounded by a world of men but was integrating into the higher echelons of the community and those who would raise the standard of living in the area. I began to feel the need for further education to keep up with the type of people I was associating with. Peter encouraged me in this and so I sat down one day and looked over the many college courses I had taken in my life starting way back with Katharine Gibbs and the Traffic Academy in New York. I had taken many courses in the nine years I was in Baltimore and had already completed several more since my return at Norwalk Community College. I put them all together and, after checking with the college about requirements for an associate degree, I decided to go back to school in earnest and earn my college degree once and for all. Almost all of my transportation and computer credits were accepted toward this goal as well as those from Katharine Gibbs and the Traffic Academy. Norwalk now gave a General Studies Degree which I could qualify for. My biggest lack was in the area of the humanities and fine arts. I had never taken any courses in music or art – not needed to become a mother trucker, I thought to myself with a smile.

Realizing that I needed six credits in humanities to get my degree, I looked into summer classes to accomplish this. In looking over what was available, I came across an overseas program being given by Fairfield University. It involved two months in Florence, Italy studying Italian Opera and Renaissance Art. These two classes would give me the humanities credits I needed to get my degree and I would get to live like an Italian for six weeks. I had taken Italian in night school before

Pat and I took our first trip to Italy ten years before. Maybe it would come back. Convincing Stuart to give me six weeks off was a totally different matter. I had five weeks vacation due me that year but I had never been allowed to take more than three at one time when I was in Traffic, and that was only when Pat and I took his mother to Italy on the QE II and Peter took pity on me.

Before doing another thing, I knew I had to get permission from Stuart. The very next morning I went into his office and closed the door. "Stuart, I need to talk to you."

"What about, Joan? You sound so serious. Is everything all right?"

"Everything's fine, Stuart. I just want to take six weeks vacation this summer to go to Italy and take my humanities courses for college." I paused to breathe and then plowed on. "I need them to get my degree and Fairfield University is going to Florence and I want to go there to do this. It is a once-in-a-lifetime opportunity and I want to take advantage of it"

Stuart sat down abruptly and looked at me astonished. "You want to go to Italy for six weeks?" he repeated. "Six weeks? You only get five weeks vacation you know. Six weeks away from the office?"

"Yes, Stuart, six weeks. The summer session is six weeks and I want to go and take two courses. The CAC's are almost dormant in the summer and Brenda can take over for me there. I'll do a newsletter just before I leave and make a summer issue good for two months. I'm sure no one will mind. I'll take the sixth week, without pay of course, and I'll work as late as you want before I go and after I get back. It's such an opportunity, Stuart. I want so much to do this. Please."

"Enough," he said. "Let me think about this a minute and I will have to run it by the president too. We report to him now, remember?"

"I remember," I answered sheepishly. "Can you let me know soon? Registration ends on Friday."

"Friday? Christ, woman, you don't give a man much time to consider, do you? I'll speak to him this afternoon and get back to you. Now, get back to work. I want the draft of the next Circle on my desk by five o'clock."

Somehow I knew I was in. It would be all right. Stuart's English bark was worse than his bite and I knew he thought this would be a great chance for me and wouldn't let me down. He didn't and by five o'clock I had his okay. I could have kissed him I was so excited.

I called Fairfield and made an appointment to go there and see if I could register for the program before the deadline. I had a choice of staying in a *pension* in the middle of Florence with the other students who were taking credit courses or staying in a hotel outside of Florence with a few other adults who were auditing courses .Before I made this decision, I called up my sister-in-law and proposed that she go with me. She was thrilled and suggested asking another of her friends to join us. My brother had no objection to her going as he had done enough Europe, he said, to last him a lifetime. Bunny and her friend, Jean, agreed that we should stay in the *pension* and rough it just like the students and so we opted for that course of action.

Before the week was up we were all registered, had paid our money and had our airline reservations made. We were to leave June 29th and start classes on the first of July. We would not be home again until August 16th. I couldn't wait to tell the girls. I hoped they would be as excited for me as I was.

We had less than three weeks to get ready and my head was swimming with thoughts of what to pack and brushing up on my Italian. It was a most exciting time. We were told that the *pension* would not be lavish and probably would not have air conditioning. We would have to walk on cobble stone streets to our classes each day so comfortable walking shoes were a must. We also found out we would have to do our own laundry – in our rooms without benefit of washing machine or dryer so we prepared the best we could. We bought a length of clothesline and lots of clothes pins and poured laundry detergent into small bottles for travelling. We hoped we thought of everything, but whatever happened, we were prepared for an adventure.

Chapter 45

We arrived in Florence early on a Monday morning and were met by a bus which took us to our home for the next six weeks. Six of our group, including the two professors assigned to be our chaperones, were dropped off at a hotel on the outskirts of town and the rest of us were delivered en masse to the *Pension Paradiso*. Bunny, Jean and I were the only adults among a group of adolescent students but we were determined to fit in. I was the only one of us who was taking the courses for credit. Bunny and Jean were here for the fun and were merely auditing.

Our room was quite large and contained three single beds, a small table and chair, a large chifferobe, which was our equivalent of a combination dresser and closet and, of all things, a bidet. This latter *accoutrement* was rather large and took up most of one corner of the room. I did know what its intended use was, but I'm sure many of the students in our group did not. Bunny and I looked at it and then at each other and in a chorus announced, "*voila* our wash tub." From that day forth, all laundry was neatly done in the bidet and hung out to dry on our brand new clothesline which we immediately hung across our room in front of the open, screenless window.

The latter became our cross to bear as we got further into the month of July when the mosquitoes became more and more prevalent in the courtyard outside our window. Also in the courtyard was a wonderful family-style *trattoria* where we met each night at six o'clock for dinner as a group. The food was delicious but, in true Italian style, there was an abundance that we were not used to. Soup was always served first, followed by a pasta course and a salad. Then the main course arrived consisting of some kind of meat, a starch, and a plethora of fresh vegetables. Hot on the heels of the entree would come a plate of fresh fruit and cheese and most nights a special dessert of some kind like a flan or bread pudding. I knew if I kept this up for six weeks I would arrive home about 50 lbs. heavier. We soon learned to pace ourselves and to decide each night between the pasta course and the meat course – but never both. I often passed up the soup altogether, or conversely made it the main part of my meal. I did this several times when I had given in to temptation and gone for a *gelato* on my way home from class.

The classes were inspiring and I was enjoying every minute of them, especially the art classes. We had a wonderful English woman as our Art Appreciation professor who we met each afternoon at the *Uffizi* Gallery. She opened up the art world for me and left me drowning in the appreciation of Renaissance Art – a style never known to me before. What a joy! I thought I had died and gone to heaven. I sucked up the knowledge like a sponge and couldn't seem to get enough.

One of the women in our group staying at the hotel also attended this class and she and I became good friends during this time which was a lucky break for me. One day as we were climbing the steps into the *Academia* for an art class, I fell. I had torn my Achilles tendon and it dropped me to the floor. The professor called a taxi and assigned an Italian speaking student to accompany me and sent me off to the local hospital. Being diagnosed in a foreign language is rather a new experience for me but I managed to understand a few words like *tendonitis* and *no camminare* (no walking) and knew I was in trouble. How was I going to get to class each day if I could not walk?

Dr. Elias, our group leader, picked up some arm crutches for me and delivered them to me at the *pension* along with some dinner She knew I could not make it to the *pension* that night for our usual meal and her thoughtfulness was much appreciated as my roommates did not even think to ask me if I needed anything, much less food. Unbelievable! With the arm crutches as walking aids and my minimal Italian I would manage. The next day, however, I struggled to get food and to get to class. My mediocre command of the Italian language stood me in fairly good stead and I was able to hobble down to the street and get a taxi to my classes on my own. Bunny and Jean were nowhere in sight, both busy with their own classes and their own interests. I was deeply hurt at the sisterly neglect but said nothing. My friend from the art class, Rena, came to my rescue. She called the Uffizi and arranged to have a wheel chair there for me. She pushed me in the wheelchair throughout the gallery and saw to it that I got back to the *tratorria* in the evening as well. She was indeed my saving grace and I was more than grateful. Not only was she a good friend and helpmate, she was very bright and a pleasure to spend time with.

The last weekend of our stay we were scheduled to go to Venice. I did not want to miss this trip as I had not seen this historic city since I visited it with Pat many years before. Bunny and Jean tried to talk me out of it, and to punctuate the foolishness of this endeavor, they assured me that I would not be staying with them and would be on my own. I was more than hurt but told them not to worry – I would manage. And I did. I got a small room on my own in the same hotel as Rena and she allowed me to tag along with her and her companion. Despite the crutches and the bad feelings I had, it was a wonderful weekend. I was able to sit in St. Mark's square and watch the crowds of people and the famous pigeons. Rena and her companion included me in their dinner plans and I did not want for friendship. They could not have been kinder and I was able to enjoy many of the sights of Venice, including a gondola ride – crutches and all.

Rena saw to it that I had a wheelchair in Rome airport and personally took me through customs and emigration on my way home from my Italian adventure. I had as little as possible to say to my traveling companions and that did not change for several months after our return from Europe. In truth, it took me a good deal of time to forgive my sister-in-law for her lack of compassion on my behalf. I did understand her motivation as it had cost a good deal of money to make this trip and she wanted to get the most out of it that she could. She had been my saving grace when I left Al and had given me food and shelter and loving care for many months. Maybe because this recent treatment seemed so unlike her was the reason for my disappointment and sadness. I never said a word to my brother but found myself too busy to visit them for some time. I did, of course, talk to Chuck on the phone, but I never let on. I'm not sure to this day if Bunny was even aware of how very much she hurt me during that difficult time.

Despite all the problems, I healed up nicely and got full credit for both courses, enabling me to get my Associate Degree after all. On May 6, 1989 I graduated from Norwalk Community College with a General Studies Degree and was as proud as any twenty-year old of my accomplishment.

My leg healed reasonably quickly after my return from Italy and life soon got back to normal. I was very busy for the first few months after my return, trying to make up for the time I had been away. One day Stuart announced that we had been given another assignment involving a lot of traveling. Dr. Stephen Covey was the new darling of the business world having just published his book called, *Seven Habits of Highly Effective People.* Stuart and I were asked by the president to take classes given by Covey at the Sundance Resort in Utah owned by Robert Redford in preparation for teaching this class to the Hitachi executives in all the branch offices as well as in the corporate office.

Having read his book from cover to cover, we were both thrilled at this news. Stuart was convinced that these classes would be invaluable to our managers and upper executives, both Japanese and American.

And so we made reservations to go to Sundance for a week to be trained as Covey facilitators. We were told to bring snow pants, boots, gloves and a light weight snow jacket as we would be doing some training outside on the mountain. I am definitely not of the athletic persuasion, so was a bit concerned about this requirement. Stuart, being a skier, was planning on including this type of attire in his suitcase, but I had to go on a shopping trip to accumulate the proper garb.

The accommodations at Sundance were most unusual. The rooms were simple wooden cabins but fitted with marvelous amenities and a view of the mountains that was breathtaking. The dining hall was comfortable and homey and produced the most wonderful meals. Photos of Robert Redford and Paul Newman as *Butch Cassidy and the Sundance Kid* were everywhere, and we felt like celebrities ourselves just being there. We had classes every morning and then again either in the afternoon or early evening. This allowed time for some outdoor activities like downhill and cross country skiing as well as some evening entertainment in the lounge.

Our outside classes turned out to be challenging but very worthwhile. We were driven up the mountain in jeeps and left there to pursue our outdoor training, which took the form of certain kinds of "games" including trust falls and leadership activities. One of the latter found us blind folded and following a group of people all holding onto the same rope led by one of the group unknown to us. It was scary to be sure but certainly did address the question of trust. I was a bit leery in the beginning but soon began to enjoy the challenges. The scenery was awesome and just being out on the mountain was an absolutely breathtaking experience. We returned to the lodge at the end of our session cold, wet and totally exhilarated. It was a wonderful week.

Chapter 46

We returned to the corporate office at the end of our week's training, totally revved up and anxious to get on the road with our dog and pony show. We were going to startle the Japanese executives with our brilliance and make everyone in our purview a smarter and wiser manager.

Before we went on the road, we gave the course to the New York Corporate Office. For me, being a facilitator was a new experience and being in front of people I worked with every day was pretty intimidating. Stu assured me I would be fine and we planned a very special program for this group. After all, the President and other important officers would be attending as well as the managers and the many hourly employees who were not used to being included in company seminars and programs.

It was still winter in New York so we had to dress warmly to fulfill the activities we had planned for the outside. Many of these were the ones we had just experienced at Sundance. Our corporate office was on seventy five acres of land so we had lots of room to set up our games, trust falls, walks and other insightful activities. We had a lot of snow on the property and some was beginning to melt so we had to instruct all participants to wear boots, as well as warm jackets and pants. For many, it was like being a kid again. I was not sure how the Japanese executives were going to take to the game portion, but I was amazed and pleased to see them volunteer for each activity and to follow Stu's instructions to the letter. He was well thought of by these executives as he was, among other things, a computer genius. The course was given in two and a half days and was a total success. We were ready to take it on the road.

The first city on our teaching circuit was Detroit. Stu and I both had a good rapport with the folks in this particular office. I was especially lucky as one of my dearest friends at HMA for many years was the office manager there. I didn't stay in a hotel as usual but stayed at Mary's home and it was great fun to get together with her again. I was also able to get her reaction to the course and answers to some questions that puzzled me.

"Are we boring them to death, Mary? Why do the Japanese men look like they're asleep – they all have their eyes closed? It's very disconcerting when you're up there giving it your all."

Mary laughed out loud. "They are not bored, Joan. That's just their way of paying very close attention. Closed eyes during a verbal presentation are considered a complement," she added. "If you notice, when you are doing an activity in which they have to participate, they are all wide awake and raring to go."

"Well, thanks for clearing that up, Mary. Stu and I were getting pretty upset, thinking they were bored out of their minds. I can't wait to tell him what you just told me. What a relief."

I passed on this information to Stu the next morning when we met for breakfast and he was as relieved as I had been. The second day went really well, and by the last day we knew we were a hit. We learned a lot this first time out – what worked and what we could do better. We were ready for our next stop which would be Chicago two months hence.

We continued facilitating this program in all the branch offices over the next year. Our last stop was the L.A. office and by the time it was over we were both pretty burned out. It was tough on both of us. Stu had to be sure the new computer system recently installed at HMA was working properly and I had to keep caught up with all the employee programs we had initiated that year as well as get out the newsletter.

Thank God I don't have a man in my life – I would never be able to get all the work done in a timely fashion, and that's what the Japanese admire and take for granted. I've never let them down before and I don't intend to start now. Being the first woman manger ever at HMA, even though there are now three, is still pretty intimidating. The best part is that I love my job *and wouldn't trade it for anything in the world.*

Stephen Covey became the watchword at HMA for the next few years and the course was given credit for an increase in business and employee productivity.

Life returned to normal for me and before I knew it, retirement was looming in the not too distant future. I decided to take stock of my situation and realized that at my present salary if I retired in April 1998, when I would be 66 years old and have 25 years of service, I would receive a very fine pension. This income, together with social security, would allow me to continue to live in the style to which I had become accustomed. It was an awesome thought.

And so I made the decision. I would retire in April 1998 and devote my time to writing the novel about my grandmother that I had always wanted to write but could never find the time. I was really getting excited about the prospect of not having to go to work ever again. I talked to Stu who assured me I would be missed but was very happy for me. I had a wonderful retirement party at which many tears were shed – twenty five years is a long time to work with many of the same people. I even received a beautiful framed going-away-thank you note (12 x 24) from Japan signed by all the managers in the overseas branches who I had known so well and worked with over the years. Several of them had become dear friends (Kirk Takahashi and Toshi Suzuki for example) and some who hosted me and a friend on a trip to the Far East where we stopped in at many of the HMA offices there. In Singapore, Ted Hiraoka played tour guide for three days, including arranging for us to have breakfast with an orangutan and her baby in the local zoo. In Hong Kong we were feted at a special dinner at a restaurant out in the harbor and taken to Macau to see the giant Buddha. These memories will remain with me forever.

I left many close friends behind who were still not eligible to retire yet, but we managed to keep in touch and share each other's lives just as we did when I was working. I took it easy and just enjoyed the spring in Connecticut and began making notes for the book, spending many hours in the local library doing research.

I developed a sudden urge to visit Florida's west coast and so I called a friend and booked my timeshare for a week in a place called Lehigh Acres. The place was just being developed then and even the main road was under construction. My friend got sick on the third day and begged to be allowed to return home. I agreed and took her to the airport the next morning. I spent the remaining week discovering the environs around me and enjoying myself as a tourist among the palm trees, lovely beaches, and nearby islands.

In January 1999 I came down with pneumonia and was very ill. Finally, I could stand it no longer and I booked myself into a condo I had seen on Pine Island while visiting southwest Florida. It was in a town called Bokelia and I went there to recuperate. I took my laptop, a tiny portable printer and all my notes and went away for a month to write my first book. I flew down and rented a car which I used only to go to church or get groceries. I really did nothing but rest and write. I drafted the entire book that month and returned home with 350 pages entitled *Julia*.

While I was in Bokelia I began to realize that I would like to consider living part time in the warmth of Florida. I fell in love with Pine Island where Bokelia was located but this area was like "old Florida" and there were almost no condos available for sale other than this one which was out of my price range. A neighbor of mine was a realtor, and after taking me to a few places in Pine Island, which we both knew were not suitable, she took me to see a condo on the Caloosahatchee River in nearby North Fort Myers. It was a small apartment on the top floor of a 5-story condo on the river. The development was called Schooner Bay and it was love at first sight. The river was like a wide silver ribbon running east and west as far as I could see. Dolphins were playing in the wakes of small boats and mullet were jumping in the calm water near the sea wall. Crab pots bobbed in the light waves and the sun made the water gleam like it was alive. All my life I had yearned to live on the water. I came close in Baltimore but never dreamed I could ever afford a place like this. I knew I had to live there, and so I closed the deal and became a Florida snowbird.

In mid-February I got a call from my thoracic surgeon who told me that the last x-ray I had turned up a lump on the right lobe of my lung. He insisted I have a biopsy as soon as possible at Stamford Hospital and I complied. The lump was a positive tumor. I had lung cancer and the decision was handed down – remove the entire right lobe of the lung. Since I had contracted emphysema ten years prior this was thought to be the wisest way to go.

There were still many tests to run and I had to clear my lungs totally of all the residue from the recent pneumonia. The surgery was set for July 21st at Stanford Hospital. All went well with the surgery and the doctor assured me that they got all the cancer. When I was stable again and back in a regular room, the doctor advised that I would not need chemo or radiation but would be checked every year from then on with a CT scan and an x-ray. I silently thanked the dear Lord, who once again was watching out for me.

I was released from the hospital on August 3rd but on August 12th I was rushed back into the hospital via ambulance and found to be severely dehydrated and bleeding from the nose uncontrollably. The latter was caused by an abscess that had formed in the empty space in my lung and got infected. I was put on antibiotics and a tube was inserted in my chest to allow the lung to drain. I was in the hospital until August 25th and went home with the tube still in place. By the time they pulled out the tube, a few weeks later, I had a permanent indentation in my chest the size of a nickel.

As soon as I thought I was on the path to recovery, there came another bump in the road. I went for my mammogram and they found a lump in my breast. In mid December I went back to the hospital for a Stereotactic procedure to remove the lump for biopsy. I told the doctor he was wasting his time and mine – it would not be cancer – one to a customer was my motto and I had already had my turn. The lump turned out to be benign. I didn't say I told you so; I just thanked God for once again being on my side.

In 2000 as soon as I was considered well enough to travel, I returned to my new condo in Florida. I spent the end of January through early April there and bought furniture and did some minimal decorating. I loved every minute of it and couldn't wait to take up residence in this paradise at the edge of the Caloosahatchee River.

The next year I came back to Florida for six months. I made quite a few friends and began to participate in some of the social activities at Schooner Bay. I was beginning to dread going home to Connecticut but missed my family and the spring season that was coming to the Northeast. It was shortly after that second trip that I decided to become a year round resident. It was becoming increasingly more difficult to breathe in the cold air of Connecticut and I could no longer walk for exercise in this beautiful state where there were so many hills. And so I took the plunge.

I decided I needed a larger unit if I was to live in Florida all year round but I also wanted to remain on the river. As luck would have it, another unit on the fourth floor became available and, without another thought, I purchased it immediately. I put my Connecticut home on the market and was fortunate to sell it in the first week. I also had to sell my fifth floor condo at Schooner Bay, so put that on the market as well. Feeling confident, I planted a statue of St. Joseph in a pot of hibiscus on my lanai and went off on a Carnival cruise with some of my Schooner Bay neighbors. "You're pretty cocky," I thought to myself.

While at sea I received a phone call from a man who put in a bid on my condo. I accepted his offer and when I came home we closed a week later. Now all I had to do was get a mover to get me from the fifth floor to the fourth. Even this turned out to be easy. Two men who worked for St. Columbkill Church (my parish) did moving on the side, and I was able to engage their services for my move. I was on a roll.

The move was more than just memorable as it occurred on September 11, 2001 – a day of infamy. A friend called me at 10:00 a.m. to see if I had heard the terrible news. I had not. I got the moving men to bring down a TV and plug it in just as the second World Trade Center tower was falling into the Manhattan streets. My excitement at moving paled in light of this unbelievable disaster. We completed the move, but the anticipation and exultant feeling of my new digs was totally overshadowed by the grim reality of 9/11.

I slowly recovered from the realization of this disaster and all its repercussions. The rest of the world did too. Though we knew our lives had been irrevocably changed forever, we all eventually got back to the business of living. It would never be the same again.

Chapter 47

Retirement suited me well, and once I got my health back, I began the toughest part of my work - editing my book. Writing I had learned was the easier of the two processes, at least for me. The story had been stored in my memory box for so many years that when I opened the box, it just poured out of me. That month in Florida produced many pages of words – no paragraphs, capitals, punctuation or grammar – just Grandma's story. Now I had to turn this cavalcade of thought into some semblance of a memoir novel. It took over two years of additional research and proofreading to accomplish this task. I also decided to fictionalize the last names just in case I had any of my historical facts not quite right. I didn't want to be sued by the Astor family, or anyone else for that matter.

When I decided it was ready, I sent the manuscript out to a few publishers. I received the requisite number of rejections and then my first acceptance. The publisher who liked *Julia* was very flattering but wanted me to make a number of changes – changes that would, in my humble opinion, turn the story into a Harlequin novel. In short, he wanted more sex and less good behavior from my heroine. I did not agree. I explained that this was a memoir based on fact and not a fiction piece. I chose to call it a novel merely to protect myself because of the prominent people included in the narrative. He was not impressed.

"If you want us to handle your book, you will have to agree to some changes," he insisted.

The changes he wanted would have turned the book into, not only an untruth, but also a racy portrait of my ancestor. Needless to say, I could not agree to these changes and adamantly refused. After much reflection, I decided to publish *Julia* myself through an online publisher who was associated with the Random House family of publishers. All in all it was a happy association and the novel was finally published in 2002.

Julia became an immediate hit as it was purchased and enjoyed by many of my friends and family who passed it on to their friends and family members. I did a good deal of marketing for this book – a chore I detested. I participated in book signings, presented at women's groups and book clubs and always had a supply of books in the trunk of my car ready to be loaned out or sold. I actually sold about 1000 copies of Julia over a three year period and still get residuals from the publisher as well as Amazon and Barnes & Nobel to this day. I must admit I am very proud of this book. I even gave it to a producer I met on Sanibel who flattered me by saying, "It's absolutely wonderful, but would cost a fortune to produce as a movie and is out of my realm of possibility." So many readers have chorused this sentiment and I have to agree, but I am satisfied that I got Julia's story out there, just as I promised her I would at her death bed.

Although I prefer to ignore them, it would be unfair of me to ignore the physical problems I was now contending with as a result of my bout with lung cancer. I had to learn to use inhalers and eventually a nebulizer in order to continue breathing sufficiently to get through each day. I learned to schedule the use of these breathing aids around my busy life schedule and even purchased a portable nebulizer so I could breathe en route in the car when necessary.

I did a fair amount of traveling in the next few years and in 2004 I decided to tackle the second book. This one would be called *Emma* and would encompass the short life of my beloved mother. *Emma* was not as easy to write as *Julia* because it brought back so many memories – some good and some very bad. Some memories I thought had been hidden away, never to raise their ugly heads again, but as the words formed in my mind and hit the screen of my computer, many tears were invoked. It was not to be completed as quickly as I had thought. Finally I completed the book in 2006 and self-published it online once again but with a different publisher this time, one who had been recommended by a fellow author friend of mine. The experience was again a pleasant one but this time I had absolutely no desire to do any marketing. I did do one or two presentations at women's groups incorporating both books in my talk but shunned signings and other public displays. It was enough to get the story told.

Emma did not sell nearly as many books as *Julia* but that was not important to me. The only reason I had for writing this book was to give my children the gift of knowing the amazing woman whom they never had the opportunity to know and love as I had. Only my eldest daughter, Elyse, had any real memories of her maternal grandmother who died so young at fifty six years old. She only had the faintest memory of her great grandmother, Julia, also but at least the book brought the memories alive. My other two daughters remembered nothing whatever about either one. As for my son, he was being born on one side of town as Emma was dying on the other. We got to show her pictures of our son in the hospital before she passed but they were never able to meet.

As soon as Emma was complete I was besieged with questions about when the next book would be published. People kept referring to them as a trilogy. The obvious subject for a third book would have to be my own life and that gave me great cause to consider. I began this daunting task in 2007 and it is still unfinished as I type these pages in the year 2010. I am not sure at this writing if I will ever actually publish the third book, but I will complete the story if I can live long enough.

Writing this book was not a labor of love but a cleansing of sorts – cathartic some might say. Some of the more sordid details are left out as I saw no useful reason to include them. I will admit that Pat was the love of my life and it took me several years of pure friendship to discover that. I'm so glad I did because I would not trade our eight years together for anything in the world. They are some of the happiest memories in my life. Our relationship taught me that real love can only be based on real friendship, and I can say unequivocally that he was the best friend I ever had. I think perhaps my two eldest daughters, when they reflect on their own marriages, will understand why I say that. They have both been blessed with friends for husbands and their unions have survived many challenges. I have wonderful memories from my liaison with Pat and very few regrets.

Although I have had several meaningful relationships over the years following my breakup with Pat, I chose to spend my life alone and have no regrets on that score. I am a firm believer that you do not need someone else to make you happy if you have learned to like yourself and your own company. There are times in our lives when our own light goes out and is rekindled by a spark from another person. Each of us has cause to think with deep gratitude of those who have lighted the flame within us. I have been so fortunate in my life in that I have made many kind and dear friends who have supported me through both the good times and the bad. My children have always been there for me whenever and wherever I needed them, and I have tried to return this care and concern at every opportunity over the years.

I wish I could have preserved and kept my family together, but I did not believe then, nor do I believe now, that this was the preferable course of action. My faith in God has always been strong and I have never felt abandoned or alone in any crisis. I am a survivor.

Where does a story truly begin? In life there are seldom clear cut beginnings – those moments when we look back and can say that everything started. Yet, there are moments when fate intersects with our daily lives, setting in motion a sequence of events whose outcome we could never have foreseen.

I think Herman Melville said it best. "Life is a voyage that is homeward bound."